Holding Companies
Complete Self-Assessment Gu

MW00389165

The guidance in this Self-Assessment is based on Holding Companies best practices and standards in business process architecture, design and quality management. The guidance is also based on the professional judgment of the individual collaborators listed in the Acknowledgments.

Notice of rights

Trademarks

Table of Contents

2

About The Art of Service

The Art of Service, Business Process Architects since 2000, is dedicated to helping stakeholders achieve excellence.

Defining, designing, creating, and implementing a process to solve a stakeholders challenge or meet an objective is the most valuable role... In EVERY group, company, organization and department.

Unless you're talking a one-time, single-use project, there should be a process. Whether that process is managed and implemented by humans, AI, or a combination of the two, it needs to be designed by someone with a complex enough perspective to ask the right questions.

Someone capable of asking the right questions and step back and say, 'What are we really trying to accomplish here? And is there a different way to look at it?'

With The Art of Service's Standard Requirements Self-Assessments, we empower people who can do just that — whether their title is marketer, entrepreneur, manager, salesperson, consultant, Business Process Manager, executive assistant, IT Manager, CIO etc... —they are the people who rule the future. They are people who watch the process as it happens, and ask the right questions to make the process work better.

Contact us when you need any support with this Self-Assessment and any help with templates, blue-prints and examples of standard documents you might need:

http://theartofservice.com
service@theartofservice.com

Included Resources - how to access

Included with your purchase of the book is the Holding

Companies Self-Assessment Spreadsheet Dashboard which contains all questions and Self-Assessment areas and auto-generates insights, graphs, and project RACI planning - all with examples to get you started right away.

How? Simply send an email to
access@theartofservice.com
with this books' title in the subject to get the Holding Companies Self Assessment Tool right away.

You will receive the following contents with New and Updated specific criteria:

• The latest quick edition of the book in PDF

• The latest complete edition of the book in PDF, which criteria correspond to the criteria in...

• The Self-Assessment Excel Dashboard, and...

• Example pre-filled Self-Assessment Excel Dashboard to get familiar with results generation

• In-depth specific Checklists covering the topic

• Project management checklists and templates to assist with implementation

INCLUDES LIFETIME SELF ASSESSMENT UPDATES

Every self assessment comes with Lifetime Updates and Lifetime Free Updated Books. Lifetime Updates is an industry-first feature which allows you to receive verified self assessment updates, ensuring you always have the most accurate information at your fingertips.

Get it now- you will be glad you did - do it now, before you forget.

Send an email to **access@theartofservice.com** with this books' title in the subject to get the Holding Companies Self Assessment Tool right away.

Purpose of this Self-Assessment

This Self-Assessment has been developed to improve understanding of the requirements and elements of Holding Companies, based on best practices and standards in business process architecture, design and quality management.

It is designed to allow for a rapid Self-Assessment to determine how closely existing management practices and procedures correspond to the elements of the Self-Assessment.

The criteria of requirements and elements of Holding Companies have been rephrased in the format of a Self-Assessment questionnaire, with a seven-criterion scoring system, as explained in this document.

In this format, even with limited background knowledge of Holding Companies, a manager can quickly review existing operations to determine how they measure up to the standards. This in turn can serve as the starting point of a 'gap analysis' to identify management tools or system elements that might usefully be implemented in the organization to help improve overall performance.

How to use the Self-Assessment

On the following pages are a series of questions to identify to what extent your Holding Companies initiative is complete in comparison to the requirements set in standards.

To facilitate answering the questions, there is a space in front of each question to enter a score on a scale of '1' to '5'.

1 Strongly Disagree

2 Disagree

3 Neutral

4 Agree

5 Strongly Agree

Read the question and rate it with the following in front of mind:

'In my belief,
the answer to this question is clearly defined'.

There are two ways in which you can choose to interpret this statement;
1. how aware are you that the answer to the question is clearly defined
2. for more in-depth analysis you can choose to gather evidence and confirm the answer to the question. This obviously will take more time, most Self-Assessment users opt for the first way to interpret the question and dig deeper later on based on the outcome of the overall Self-Assessment.

A score of '1' would mean that the answer is not clear at all, where a '5' would mean the answer is crystal clear and defined. Leave emtpy when the question is not applicable or you don't want to answer it, you can skip it without affecting your score. Write your score in the space provided.

After you have responded to all the appropriate statements in each section, compute your average score for that section, using the formula provided, and round to the nearest tenth. Then transfer to the corresponding spoke in the Holding Companies Scorecard on the second next page of the Self-Assessment.

Your completed Holding Companies Scorecard will give you a clear presentation of which Holding Companies areas need attention.

Holding Companies
Scorecard Example

Example of how the finalized Scorecard can look like:

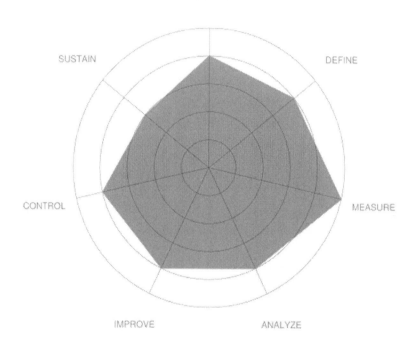

Holding Companies
Scorecard

Your Scores:

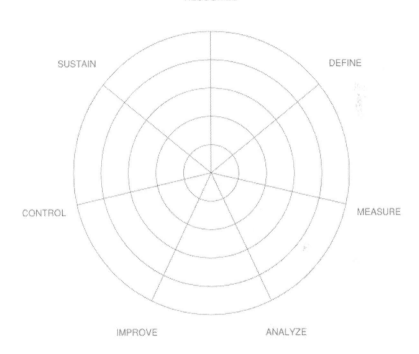

BEGINNING OF THE SELF-ASSESSMENT:

CRITERION #1: RECOGNIZE

INTENT: Be aware of the need for change. Recognize that there is an unfavorable variation, problem or symptom.

In my belief, the answer to this question is clearly defined:

5 Strongly Agree

4 Agree

3 Neutral

2 Disagree

1 Strongly Disagree

1. Will new equipment/products be required to facilitate Holding companies delivery, for example is new software needed?
<--- Score

2. Who needs what information?
<--- Score

3. What are the Holding companies resources needed?

<--- Score

4. Looking at each person individually – does every one have the qualities which are needed to work in this group?
<--- Score

5. What needs to be done?
<--- Score

6. To what extent would your organization benefit from being recognized as a award recipient?
<--- Score

7. Think about the people you identified for your Holding companies project and the project responsibilities you would assign to them, what kind of training do you think they would need to perform these responsibilities effectively?
<--- Score

8. Are employees recognized for desired behaviors?
<--- Score

9. How do you identify the kinds of information that you will need?
<--- Score

10. What is the recognized need?
<--- Score

11. Are there Holding companies problems defined?
<--- Score

12. What should be considered when identifying available resources, constraints, and deadlines?

<--- Score

13. Are your goals realistic? Do you need to redefine your problem? Perhaps the problem has changed or maybe you have reached your goal and need to set a new one?
<--- Score

14. What Holding companies coordination do you need?
<--- Score

15. What are the clients issues and concerns?
<--- Score

16. How do you identify subcontractor relationships?
<--- Score

17. Do you have/need 24-hour access to key personnel?
<--- Score

18. Does the problem have ethical dimensions?
<--- Score

19. Is it clear when you think of the day ahead of you what activities and tasks you need to complete?
<--- Score

20. What situation(s) led to this Holding companies Self Assessment?
<--- Score

21. As a sponsor, customer or management, how important is it to meet goals, objectives?
<--- Score

22. What problems are you facing and how do you consider Holding companies will circumvent those obstacles?
<--- Score

23. What are the stakeholder objectives to be achieved with Holding companies?
<--- Score

24. For your Holding companies project, identify and describe the business environment, is there more than one layer to the business environment?
<--- Score

25. Do you need to avoid or amend any Holding companies activities?
<--- Score

26. Do you recognize Holding companies achievements?
<--- Score

27. Where is training needed?
<--- Score

28. Which needs are not included or involved?
<--- Score

29. Is the need for organizational change recognized?
<--- Score

30. Why is this needed?
<--- Score

31. Will a response program recognize when a crisis

occurs and provide some level of response?
<--- Score

32. Which issues are too important to ignore?
<--- Score

33. What prevents you from making the changes you know will make you a more effective Holding companies leader?
<--- Score

34. Who are your key stakeholders who need to sign off?
<--- Score

35. Is the quality assurance team identified?
<--- Score

36. What vendors make products that address the Holding companies needs?
<--- Score

37. Who needs to know about Holding companies?
<--- Score

38. What Holding companies events should you attend?
<--- Score

39. Is it needed?
<--- Score

40. What Holding companies capabilities do you need?
<--- Score

41. Who else hopes to benefit from it?
<--- Score

42. What Holding companies problem should be solved?
<--- Score

43. What needs to stay?
<--- Score

44. How many trainings, in total, are needed?
<--- Score

45. Are controls defined to recognize and contain problems?
<--- Score

46. Can management personnel recognize the monetary benefit of Holding companies?
<--- Score

47. How much are sponsors, customers, partners, stakeholders involved in Holding companies? In other words, what are the risks, if Holding companies does not deliver successfully?
<--- Score

48. Who should resolve the Holding companies issues?
<--- Score

49. Who defines the rules in relation to any given issue?
<--- Score

50. How can auditing be a preventative security

measure?
<--- Score

51. What is the problem or issue?
<--- Score

52. What would happen if Holding companies weren't done?
<--- Score

53. What does Holding companies success mean to the stakeholders?
<--- Score

54. Will it solve real problems?
<--- Score

55. Are losses recognized in a timely manner?
<--- Score

56. What else needs to be measured?
<--- Score

57. How are you going to measure success?
<--- Score

58. Does your organization need more Holding companies education?
<--- Score

59. What is the smallest subset of the problem you can usefully solve?
<--- Score

60. Do you know what you need to know about Holding companies?

<--- Score

61. Are employees recognized or rewarded for performance that demonstrates the highest levels of integrity?
<--- Score

62. Who needs budgets?
<--- Score

63. What do you need to start doing?
<--- Score

64. How do you assess your Holding companies workforce capability and capacity needs, including skills, competencies, and staffing levels?
<--- Score

65. Where do you need to exercise leadership?
<--- Score

66. What tools and technologies are needed for a custom Holding companies project?
<--- Score

67. What are your needs in relation to Holding companies skills, labor, equipment, and markets?
<--- Score

68. What is the extent or complexity of the Holding companies problem?
<--- Score

69. How do you take a forward-looking perspective in identifying Holding companies research related to market response and models?

<--- Score

70. What resources or support might you need?
<--- Score

71. What activities does the governance board need
to consider?
<--- Score

72. What do employees need in the short term?
<--- Score

73. Do you need different information or graphics?
<--- Score

74. What creative shifts do you need to take?
<--- Score

75. Are you dealing with any of the same issues today
as yesterday? What can you do about this?
<--- Score

76. Are problem definition and motivation clearly
presented?
<--- Score

77. Are there any specific expectations or concerns
about the Holding companies team, Holding
companies itself?
<--- Score

78. How are training requirements identified?
<--- Score

79. What are the minority interests and what amount
of minority interests can be recognized?

<--- Score

80. Did you miss any major Holding companies issues?
<--- Score

81. What training and capacity building actions are needed to implement proposed reforms?
<--- Score

82. Would you recognize a threat from the inside?
<--- Score

83. What is the Holding companies problem definition? What do you need to resolve?
<--- Score

84. Are there regulatory / compliance issues?
<--- Score

85. How do you recognize an Holding companies objection?
<--- Score

86. Does Holding companies create potential expectations in other areas that need to be recognized and considered?
<--- Score

87. How do you recognize an objection?
<--- Score

88. What are the expected benefits of Holding companies to the stakeholder?
<--- Score

89. How are the Holding companies's objectives

aligned to the group's overall stakeholder strategy?
<--- Score

90. What is the problem and/or vulnerability?
<--- Score

91. Which information does the Holding companies business case need to include?
<--- Score

92. Will Holding companies deliverables need to be tested and, if so, by whom?
<--- Score

93. Why the need?
<--- Score

94. Consider your own Holding companies project, what types of organizational problems do you think might be causing or affecting your problem, based on the work done so far?
<--- Score

95. What extra resources will you need?
<--- Score

Add up total points for this section:
_ _ _ _ _ = Total points for this section

Divided by: _ _ _ _ _ _ (number of
statements answered) = _ _ _ _ _ _
Average score for this section

Transfer your score to the Holding
companies Index at the beginning of the
Self-Assessment.

CRITERION #2: DEFINE:

INTENT: Formulate the stakeholder problem. Define the problem, needs and objectives.

In my belief, the answer to this question is clearly defined:

5 Strongly Agree

4 Agree

3 Neutral

2 Disagree

1 Strongly Disagree

1. What is the scope of the Holding companies work?
<--- Score

2. What are the compelling stakeholder reasons for embarking on Holding companies?
<--- Score

3. How do you manage changes in Holding companies requirements?

<--- Score

4. Has the Holding companies work been fairly and/
or equitably divided and delegated among team
members who are qualified and capable to perform
the work? Has everyone contributed?
<--- Score

5. Are resources adequate for the scope?
<--- Score

6. What specifically is the problem? Where does it
occur? When does it occur? What is its extent?
<--- Score

7. Is the Holding companies scope manageable?
<--- Score

8. What knowledge or experience is required?
<--- Score

9. What is the definition of success?
<--- Score

10. What is the scope?
<--- Score

11. Is there a completed, verified, and validated high-
level 'as is' (not 'should be' or 'could be') stakeholder
process map?
<--- Score

12. How was the 'as is' process map developed,
reviewed, verified and validated?
<--- Score

13. How does the Holding companies manager ensure against scope creep?
<--- Score

14. Is scope creep really all bad news?
<--- Score

15. Have all basic functions of Holding companies been defined?
<--- Score

16. Who approved the Holding companies scope?
<--- Score

17. What are the Holding companies use cases?
<--- Score

18. Are required metrics defined, what are they?
<--- Score

19. What critical content must be communicated – who, what, when, where, and how?
<--- Score

20. How will variation in the actual durations of each activity be dealt with to ensure that the expected Holding companies results are met?
<--- Score

21. What are the Holding companies tasks and definitions?
<--- Score

22. Who are the Holding companies improvement team members, including Management Leads and Coaches?

<--- Score

23. Is there a critical path to deliver Holding companies results?
<--- Score

24. Are task requirements clearly defined?
<--- Score

25. What is the scope of Holding companies?
<--- Score

26. What key stakeholder process output measure(s) does Holding companies leverage and how?
<--- Score

27. How do you catch Holding companies definition inconsistencies?
<--- Score

28. When is the estimated completion date?
<--- Score

29. How do you build the right business case?
<--- Score

30. Is the current 'as is' process being followed? If not, what are the discrepancies?
<--- Score

31. How and when will the baselines be defined?
<--- Score

32. What are the record-keeping requirements of Holding companies activities?
<--- Score

33. Has the direction changed at all during the course of Holding companies? If so, when did it change and why?
<--- Score

34. Has a team charter been developed and communicated?
<--- Score

35. What are the boundaries of the scope? What is in bounds and what is not? What is the start point? What is the stop point?
<--- Score

36. What is out of scope?
<--- Score

37. What is in scope?
<--- Score

38. Has everyone on the team, including the team leaders, been properly trained?
<--- Score

39. Do you have organizational privacy requirements?
<--- Score

40. Are there any constraints known that bear on the ability to perform Holding companies work? How is the team addressing them?
<--- Score

41. Do you have a Holding companies success story or case study ready to tell and share?
<--- Score

42. What is the context?
<--- Score

43. How do you gather the stories?
<--- Score

44. What defines best in class?
<--- Score

45. What Holding companies requirements should be gathered?
<--- Score

46. What sources do you use to gather information for a Holding companies study?
<--- Score

47. Who defines (or who defined) the rules and roles?
<--- Score

48. Is Holding companies linked to key stakeholder goals and objectives?
<--- Score

49. Are audit criteria, scope, frequency and methods defined?
<--- Score

50. Have specific policy objectives been defined?
<--- Score

51. Is there a Holding companies management charter, including stakeholder case, problem and goal statements, scope, milestones, roles and responsibilities, communication plan?

<--- Score

52. The political context: who holds power?
<--- Score

53. When are meeting minutes sent out? Who is on the distribution list?
<--- Score

54. What are the rough order estimates on cost savings/opportunities that Holding companies brings?
<--- Score

55. What system do you use for gathering Holding companies information?
<--- Score

56. How do you manage unclear Holding companies requirements?
<--- Score

57. How often are the team meetings?
<--- Score

58. What Holding companies services do you require?
<--- Score

59. Are different versions of process maps needed to account for the different types of inputs?
<--- Score

60. What customer feedback methods were used to solicit their input?
<--- Score

61. Has a project plan, Gantt chart, or similar been developed/completed?
<--- Score

62. What are the dynamics of the communication plan?
<--- Score

63. Is the work to date meeting requirements?
<--- Score

64. Does the scope remain the same?
<--- Score

65. Is there regularly 100% attendance at the team meetings? If not, have appointed substitutes attended to preserve cross-functionality and full representation?
<--- Score

66. Is the improvement team aware of the different versions of a process: what they think it is vs. what it actually is vs. what it should be vs. what it could be?
<--- Score

67. Do you all define Holding companies in the same way?
<--- Score

68. What is the definition of Holding companies excellence?
<--- Score

69. How is the team tracking and documenting its work?
<--- Score

70. Is data collected and displayed to better understand customer(s) critical needs and requirements.
<--- Score

71. Are the Holding companies requirements testable?
<--- Score

72. In what way can you redefine the criteria of choice clients have in your category in your favor?
<--- Score

73. How have you defined all Holding companies requirements first?
<--- Score

74. Are there different segments of customers?
<--- Score

75. How would you define Holding companies leadership?
<--- Score

76. How do you think the partners involved in Holding companies would have defined success?
<--- Score

77. What is in the scope and what is not in scope?
<--- Score

78. Has a high-level 'as is' process map been completed, verified and validated?
<--- Score

79. Will a Holding companies production readiness review be required?
<--- Score

80. What are the Roles and Responsibilities for each team member and its leadership? Where is this documented?
<--- Score

81. What sort of initial information to gather?
<--- Score

82. Who is gathering Holding companies information?
<--- Score

83. Are approval levels defined for contracts and supplements to contracts?
<--- Score

84. What intelligence can you gather?
<--- Score

85. How are consistent Holding companies definitions important?
<--- Score

86. What gets examined?
<--- Score

87. Has/have the customer(s) been identified?
<--- Score

88. How do you keep key subject matter experts in the loop?
<--- Score

89. What are the core elements of the Holding companies business case?
<--- Score

90. What is the scope of the Holding companies effort?
<--- Score

91. How can the value of Holding companies be defined?
<--- Score

92. How do you gather requirements?
<--- Score

93. Who is gathering information?
<--- Score

94. Are all requirements met?
<--- Score

95. Is the Holding companies scope complete and appropriately sized?
<--- Score

96. What are (control) requirements for Holding companies Information?
<--- Score

97. What is the worst case scenario?
<--- Score

98. Are accountability and ownership for Holding companies clearly defined?
<--- Score

99. How do you gather Holding companies requirements?
<--- Score

100. Is there a completed SIPOC representation, describing the Suppliers, Inputs, Process, Outputs, and Customers?
<--- Score

101. What would be the goal or target for a Holding companies's improvement team?
<--- Score

102. Is the scope of Holding companies defined?
<--- Score

103. What baselines are required to be defined and managed?
<--- Score

104. Why are you doing Holding companies and what is the scope?
<--- Score

105. How will the Holding companies team and the group measure complete success of Holding companies?
<--- Score

106. Has anyone else (internal or external to the group) attempted to solve this problem or a similar one before? If so, what knowledge can be leveraged from these previous efforts?
<--- Score

107. Do the problem and goal statements meet the

SMART criteria (specific, measurable, attainable, relevant, and time-bound)?

<--- Score

108. How would you define the culture at your organization, how susceptible is it to Holding companies changes?

<--- Score

109. What scope to assess?

<--- Score

110. What are the tasks and definitions?

<--- Score

111. Have all of the relationships been defined properly?

<--- Score

112. What is out-of-scope initially?

<--- Score

113. What information do you gather?

<--- Score

114. What are the requirements for audit information?

<--- Score

115. Is there any additional Holding companies definition of success?

<--- Score

116. When is/was the Holding companies start date?

<--- Score

117. Are roles and responsibilities formally defined?

<--- Score

118. What is a worst-case scenario for losses?
<--- Score

119. Are the Holding companies requirements complete?
<--- Score

120. How do you manage scope?
<--- Score

121. Is the team adequately staffed with the desired cross-functionality? If not, what additional resources are available to the team?
<--- Score

122. Is there a clear Holding companies case definition?
<--- Score

123. Does the team have regular meetings?
<--- Score

124. Is Holding companies required?
<--- Score

125. How do you hand over Holding companies context?
<--- Score

126. How did the Holding companies manager receive input to the development of a Holding companies improvement plan and the estimated completion dates/times of each activity?
<--- Score

127. If substitutes have been appointed, have they been briefed on the Holding companies goals and received regular communications as to the progress to date?
<--- Score

128. Is Holding companies currently on schedule according to the plan?
<--- Score

129. What was the context?
<--- Score

130. Is it clearly defined in and to your organization what you do?
<--- Score

131. What constraints exist that might impact the team?
<--- Score

132. Have the customer needs been translated into specific, measurable requirements? How?
<--- Score

133. Scope of sensitive information?
<--- Score

134. Has your scope been defined?
<--- Score

135. Has the improvement team collected the 'voice of the customer' (obtained feedback – qualitative and quantitative)?
<--- Score

136. What scope do you want your strategy to cover?
<--- Score

Add up total points for this section:
_____ = Total points for this section

Divided by: _____ (number of
statements answered) = _____
Average score for this section

Transfer your score to the Holding
companies Index at the beginning of the
Self-Assessment.

CRITERION #3: MEASURE:

INTENT: Gather the correct data.
Measure the current performance and
evolution of the situation.

In my belief, the answer to this
question is clearly defined:

5 Strongly Agree

4 Agree

3 Neutral

2 Disagree

1 Strongly Disagree

1. What are the operational costs after Holding
companies deployment?
<--- Score

2. What are the strategic priorities for this year?
<--- Score

3. Does a Holding companies quantification method
exist?

<--- Score

4. How do you measure efficient delivery of Holding companies services?
<--- Score

5. Which Holding companies impacts are significant?
<--- Score

6. What are allowable costs?
<--- Score

7. Are supply costs steady or fluctuating?
<--- Score

8. Have you made assumptions about the shape of the future, particularly its impact on your customers and competitors?
<--- Score

9. Is it possible to estimate the impact of unanticipated complexity such as wrong or failed assumptions, feedback, etcetera on proposed reforms?
<--- Score

10. Why do you expend time and effort to implement measurement, for whom?
<--- Score

11. What are the current costs of the Holding companies process?
<--- Score

12. Do you have any cost Holding companies limitation requirements?

<--- Score

13. Are there measurements based on task performance?
<--- Score

14. How do you control the overall costs of your work processes?
<--- Score

15. When are costs are incurred?
<--- Score

16. What do you measure and why?
<--- Score

17. What happens if cost savings do not materialize?
<--- Score

18. Are missed Holding companies opportunities costing your organization money?
<--- Score

19. How do you measure variability?
<--- Score

20. Do the benefits outweigh the costs?
<--- Score

21. What causes mismanagement?
<--- Score

22. What can be used to verify compliance?
<--- Score

23. What does a Test Case verify?

<--- Score

24. Are there any easy-to-implement alternatives to Holding companies? Sometimes other solutions are available that do not require the cost implications of a full-blown project?
<--- Score

25. How do you measure lifecycle phases?
<--- Score

26. What drives O&M cost?
<--- Score

27. How much does it cost?
<--- Score

28. What would it cost to replace your technology?
<--- Score

29. Are the Holding companies benefits worth its costs?
<--- Score

30. How can you measure Holding companies in a systematic way?
<--- Score

31. What disadvantage does this cause for the user?
<--- Score

32. Do you have a flow diagram of what happens?
<--- Score

33. Are you aware of what could cause a problem?
<--- Score

34. Where is the cost?
<--- Score

35. When should you bother with diagrams?
<--- Score

36. Do you have an issue in getting priority?
<--- Score

37. What are the uncertainties surrounding estimates of impact?
<--- Score

38. Are you taking your company in the direction of better and revenue or cheaper and cost?
<--- Score

39. What tests verify requirements?
<--- Score

40. What are the costs of delaying Holding companies action?
<--- Score

41. How can a Holding companies test verify your ideas or assumptions?
<--- Score

42. How long to keep data and how to manage retention costs?
<--- Score

43. What is the cost of rework?
<--- Score

44. How can you reduce the costs of obtaining inputs?
<--- Score

45. How do you verify and validate the Holding companies data?
<--- Score

46. How to cause the change?
<--- Score

47. Have you included everything in your Holding companies cost models?
<--- Score

48. How do you aggregate measures across priorities?
<--- Score

49. What do people want to verify?
<--- Score

50. What is the Holding companies business impact?
<--- Score

51. What are hidden Holding companies quality costs?
<--- Score

52. What are the estimated costs of proposed changes?
<--- Score

53. How sensitive must the Holding companies strategy be to cost?
<--- Score

54. Who is involved in verifying compliance?
<--- Score

55. What is an unallowable cost?
<--- Score

56. Did you tackle the cause or the symptom?
<--- Score

57. Does management have the right priorities among projects?
<--- Score

58. How will success or failure be measured?
<--- Score

59. What are your customers expectations and measures?
<--- Score

60. What measurements are being captured?
<--- Score

61. What could cause you to change course?
<--- Score

62. What are your operating costs?
<--- Score

63. What is your decision requirements diagram?
<--- Score

64. How will your organization measure success?
<--- Score

65. What does verifying compliance entail?
<--- Score

66. What causes innovation to fail or succeed in your organization?
<--- Score

67. What is measured? Why?
<--- Score

68. What methods are feasible and acceptable to estimate the impact of reforms?
<--- Score

69. How are costs allocated?
<--- Score

70. Among the Holding companies product and service cost to be estimated, which is considered hardest to estimate?
<--- Score

71. Do you effectively measure and reward individual and team performance?
<--- Score

72. What are you verifying?
<--- Score

73. What are the Holding companies investment costs?
<--- Score

74. Will Holding companies have an impact on current business continuity, disaster recovery processes and/ or infrastructure?
<--- Score

75. What is your Holding companies quality cost

segregation study?

<--- Score

76. Which costs should be taken into account?

<--- Score

77. How do you verify your resources?

<--- Score

78. How will effects be measured?

<--- Score

79. Are there competing Holding companies priorities?

<--- Score

80. How do you verify performance?

<--- Score

81. How is the value delivered by Holding companies being measured?

<--- Score

82. What is the total fixed cost?

<--- Score

83. What would be a real cause for concern?

<--- Score

84. How is performance measured?

<--- Score

85. What evidence is there and what is measured?

<--- Score

86. What could cause delays in the schedule?

<--- Score

87. Has a cost center been established?
<--- Score

88. How can you measure the performance?
<--- Score

89. Are you able to realize any cost savings?
<--- Score

90. How do you verify and develop ideas and innovations?
<--- Score

91. What does your operating model cost?
<--- Score

92. What are the costs of reform?
<--- Score

93. What are the costs?
<--- Score

94. Where is it measured?
<--- Score

95. Do you aggressively reward and promote the people who have the biggest impact on creating excellent Holding companies services/products?
<--- Score

96. How will you measure your Holding companies effectiveness?
<--- Score

97. How can you reduce costs?
<--- Score

98. Was a business case (cost/benefit) developed?
<--- Score

99. How frequently do you track Holding companies measures?
<--- Score

100. Are indirect costs charged to the Holding companies program?
<--- Score

101. What harm might be caused?
<--- Score

102. Which measures and indicators matter?
<--- Score

103. What relevant entities could be measured?
<--- Score

104. What does losing customers cost your organization?
<--- Score

105. How can you manage cost down?
<--- Score

106. What are your key Holding companies organizational performance measures, including key short and longer-term financial measures?
<--- Score

107. What are the types and number of measures to

use?

<--- Score

108. What is the cause of any Holding companies gaps?

<--- Score

109. Are the units of measure consistent?

<--- Score

110. What is the root cause(s) of the problem?

<--- Score

111. How will costs be allocated?

<--- Score

112. What causes investor action?

<--- Score

113. How do you prevent mis-estimating cost?

<--- Score

114. How are measurements made?

<--- Score

115. What users will be impacted?

<--- Score

116. Are Holding companies vulnerabilities categorized and prioritized?

<--- Score

117. How do you quantify and qualify impacts?

<--- Score

118. Are actual costs in line with budgeted costs?

<--- Score

119. Are the measurements objective?
<--- Score

120. What measurements are possible, practicable and meaningful?
<--- Score

121. How will you measure success?
<--- Score

122. Have design-to-cost goals been established?
<--- Score

123. How do your measurements capture actionable Holding companies information for use in exceeding your customers expectations and securing your customers engagement?
<--- Score

124. When a disaster occurs, who gets priority?
<--- Score

125. How is progress measured?
<--- Score

126. Do you verify that corrective actions were taken?
<--- Score

127. How will measures be used to manage and adapt?
<--- Score

128. Is the cost worth the Holding companies effort ?
<--- Score

129. Is there an opportunity to verify requirements?
<--- Score

130. Who should receive measurement reports?
<--- Score

131. Where can you go to verify the info?
<--- Score

Add up total points for this section:
_ _ _ _ _ = Total points for this section

Divided by: _ _ _ _ _ _ (number of
statements answered) = _ _ _ _ _ _
Average score for this section

Transfer your score to the Holding
companies Index at the beginning of the
Self-Assessment.

CRITERION #4: ANALYZE:

INTENT: Analyze causes, assumptions and hypotheses.

In my belief, the answer to this question is clearly defined:

5 Strongly Agree

4 Agree

3 Neutral

2 Disagree

1 Strongly Disagree

1. What does the data say about the performance of the stakeholder process?
<--- Score

2. What qualifications and skills do you need?
<--- Score

3. Has an output goal been set?
<--- Score

4. What are your Holding companies processes?
<--- Score

5. Do you have the authority to produce the output?
<--- Score

6. What process improvements will be needed?
<--- Score

7. What types of data do your Holding companies indicators require?
<--- Score

8. Who qualifies to gain access to data?
<--- Score

9. What did the team gain from developing a sub-process map?
<--- Score

10. What internal processes need improvement?
<--- Score

11. What are the best opportunities for value improvement?
<--- Score

12. What qualifications are needed?
<--- Score

13. What systems/processes must you excel at?
<--- Score

14. What were the financial benefits resulting from any 'ground fruit or low-hanging fruit' (quick fixes)?
<--- Score

15. Is pre-qualification of suppliers carried out?
<--- Score

16. Do your contracts/agreements contain data security obligations?
<--- Score

17. How will the Holding companies data be captured?
<--- Score

18. What is your organizations process which leads to recognition of value generation?
<--- Score

19. What are evaluation criteria for the output?
<--- Score

20. Is there a strict change management process?
<--- Score

21. What is the Holding companies Driver?
<--- Score

22. Have you defined which data is gathered how?
<--- Score

23. What are the necessary qualifications?
<--- Score

24. What is the Value Stream Mapping?
<--- Score

25. What are the revised rough estimates of the financial savings/opportunity for Holding companies

improvements?
<--- Score

26. A compounding model resolution with available relevant data can often provide insight towards a solution methodology; which Holding companies models, tools and techniques are necessary?
<--- Score

27. Where can you get qualified talent today?
<--- Score

28. Who is involved in the management review process?
<--- Score

29. Was a detailed process map created to amplify critical steps of the 'as is' stakeholder process?
<--- Score

30. How is data used for program management and improvement?
<--- Score

31. Think about the functions involved in your Holding companies project, what processes flow from these functions?
<--- Score

32. What are your best practices for minimizing Holding companies project risk, while demonstrating incremental value and quick wins throughout the Holding companies project lifecycle?
<--- Score

33. How much data can be collected in the given

timeframe?
<--- Score

34. How does the organization define, manage, and improve its Holding companies processes?
<--- Score

35. What are the processes for audit reporting and management?
<--- Score

36. Record-keeping requirements flow from the records needed as inputs, outputs, controls and for transformation of a Holding companies process, are the records needed as inputs to the Holding companies process available?
<--- Score

37. How do you ensure that the Holding companies opportunity is realistic?
<--- Score

38. What is the oversight process?
<--- Score

39. How is the way you as the leader think and process information affecting your organizational culture?
<--- Score

40. What methods do you use to gather Holding companies data?
<--- Score

41. How many input/output points does it require?
<--- Score

42. Were there any improvement opportunities identified from the process analysis?
<--- Score

43. Identify an operational issue in your organization, for example, could a particular task be done more quickly or more efficiently by Holding companies?
<--- Score

44. What are the personnel training and qualifications required?
<--- Score

45. How will corresponding data be collected?
<--- Score

46. Are you missing Holding companies opportunities?
<--- Score

47. What are your current levels and trends in key Holding companies measures or indicators of product and process performance that are important to and directly serve your customers?
<--- Score

48. An organizationally feasible system request is one that considers the mission, goals and objectives of the organization, key questions are: is the Holding companies solution request practical and will it solve a problem or take advantage of an opportunity to achieve company goals?
<--- Score

49. Who will gather what data?
<--- Score

50. What data is gathered?
<--- Score

51. What other organizational variables, such as reward systems or communication systems, affect the performance of this Holding companies process?
<--- Score

52. What Holding companies data will be collected?
<--- Score

53. How do you identify specific Holding companies investment opportunities and emerging trends?
<--- Score

54. What data do you need to collect?
<--- Score

55. What Holding companies metrics are outputs of the process?
<--- Score

56. How is Holding companies data gathered?
<--- Score

57. What tools were used to narrow the list of possible causes?
<--- Score

58. Is data and process analysis, root cause analysis and quantifying the gap/opportunity in place?
<--- Score

59. What successful thing are you doing today that may be blinding you to new growth opportunities?

<--- Score

60. What are your current levels and trends in key measures or indicators of Holding companies product and process performance that are important to and directly serve your customers? How do these results compare with the performance of your competitors and other organizations with similar offerings?
<--- Score

61. Has data output been validated?
<--- Score

62. How do you promote understanding that opportunity for improvement is not criticism of the status quo, or the people who created the status quo?
<--- Score

63. Is there any way to speed up the process?
<--- Score

64. Can you add value to the current Holding companies decision-making process (largely qualitative) by incorporating uncertainty modeling (more quantitative)?
<--- Score

65. Is the gap/opportunity displayed and communicated in financial terms?
<--- Score

66. What tools were used to generate the list of possible causes?
<--- Score

67. Where is Holding companies data gathered?

<--- Score

68. What qualifies as competition?
<--- Score

69. Do your employees have the opportunity to do
what they do best everyday?
<--- Score

70. What kind of crime could a potential new hire
have committed that would not only not disqualify
him/her from being hired by your organization,
but would actually indicate that he/she might be a
particularly good fit?
<--- Score

71. What is the complexity of the output produced?
<--- Score

72. How do you implement and manage your
work processes to ensure that they meet design
requirements?
<--- Score

73. What are the Holding companies business drivers?
<--- Score

74. Do you understand your management processes
today?
<--- Score

75. How is the Holding companies Value Stream
Mapping managed?
<--- Score

76. What are the disruptive Holding companies

technologies that enable your organization to radically change your business processes?
<--- Score

77. Who will facilitate the team and process?
<--- Score

78. How do you define collaboration and team output?
<--- Score

79. Do your leaders quickly bounce back from setbacks?
<--- Score

80. Is the suppliers process defined and controlled?
<--- Score

81. Do staff qualifications match your project?
<--- Score

82. Is the final output clearly identified?
<--- Score

83. Is the performance gap determined?
<--- Score

84. How has the Holding companies data been gathered?
<--- Score

85. Do quality systems drive continuous improvement?
<--- Score

86. What, related to, Holding companies processes

does your organization outsource?

<--- Score

87. How often will data be collected for measures?

<--- Score

88. What training and qualifications will you need?

<--- Score

89. What is holding companies from transitioning to open source data integration?

<--- Score

90. What Holding companies data should be managed?

<--- Score

91. Are all staff in core Holding companies subjects Highly Qualified?

<--- Score

92. Think about some of the processes you undertake within your organization, which do you own?

<--- Score

93. What information qualified as important?

<--- Score

94. Are Holding companies changes recognized early enough to be approved through the regular process?

<--- Score

95. How are outputs preserved and protected?

<--- Score

96. How do your work systems and key work

processes relate to and capitalize on your core competencies?
<--- Score

97. Where is the data coming from to measure compliance?
<--- Score

98. How difficult is it to qualify what Holding companies ROI is?
<--- Score

99. Do you, as a leader, bounce back quickly from setbacks?
<--- Score

100. What controls do you have in place to protect data?
<--- Score

101. What quality tools were used to get through the analyze phase?
<--- Score

102. What are your outputs?
<--- Score

103. What other jobs or tasks affect the performance of the steps in the Holding companies process?
<--- Score

104. What is the cost of poor quality as supported by the team's analysis?
<--- Score

105. Is the required Holding companies data

gathered?
<--- Score

106. When should a process be art not science?
<--- Score

107. Are your outputs consistent?
<--- Score

108. What is the output?
<--- Score

109. Should you invest in industry-recognized qualifications?
<--- Score

110. How do you measure the operational performance of your key work systems and processes, including productivity, cycle time, and other appropriate measures of process effectiveness, efficiency, and innovation?
<--- Score

111. What qualifications are necessary?
<--- Score

112. Was a cause-and-effect diagram used to explore the different types of causes (or sources of variation)?
<--- Score

113. What qualifications do Holding companies leaders need?
<--- Score

114. How will the data be checked for quality?
<--- Score

115. What conclusions were drawn from the team's data collection and analysis? How did the team reach these conclusions?
<--- Score

116. What Holding companies data do you gather or use now?
<--- Score

117. Do several people in different organizational units assist with the Holding companies process?
<--- Score

118. How was the detailed process map generated, verified, and validated?
<--- Score

119. Are all team members qualified for all tasks?
<--- Score

120. What will drive Holding companies change?
<--- Score

121. Who gets your output?
<--- Score

122. What are the Holding companies design outputs?
<--- Score

123. What resources go in to get the desired output?
<--- Score

124. What were the crucial 'moments of truth' on the process map?
<--- Score

125. What output to create?
<--- Score

126. How will the change process be managed?
<--- Score

127. What is your organizations system for selecting qualified vendors?
<--- Score

128. Were Pareto charts (or similar) used to portray the 'heavy hitters' (or key sources of variation)?
<--- Score

129. What are your key performance measures or indicators and in-process measures for the control and improvement of your Holding companies processes?
<--- Score

130. Is the Holding companies process severely broken such that a re-design is necessary?
<--- Score

131. Who owns what data?
<--- Score

132. How do mission and objectives affect the Holding companies processes of your organization?
<--- Score

133. What process should you select for improvement?
<--- Score

134. Were any designed experiments used to generate additional insight into the data analysis?
<--- Score

Add up total points for this section:
_____ = Total points for this section

Divided by: _____ (number of statements answered) = _____
Average score for this section

Transfer your score to the Holding companies Index at the beginning of the Self-Assessment.

CRITERION #5: IMPROVE:

INTENT: Develop a practical solution.
Innovate, establish and test the
solution and to measure the results.

In my belief, the answer to this
question is clearly defined:

5 Strongly Agree

4 Agree

3 Neutral

2 Disagree

1 Strongly Disagree

1. Who are the Holding companies decision makers?
<--- Score

2. How do you improve productivity?
<--- Score

3. How can you improve performance?
<--- Score

4. Do you cover the five essential competencies: Communication, Collaboration,Innovation, Adaptability, and Leadership that improve an organizations ability to leverage the new Holding companies in a volatile global economy?
<--- Score

5. How do you improve Holding companies service perception, and satisfaction?
<--- Score

6. How do you deal with Holding companies risk?
<--- Score

7. How do the Holding companies results compare with the performance of your competitors and other organizations with similar offerings?
<--- Score

8. How do you measure progress and evaluate training effectiveness?
<--- Score

9. Have you identified breakpoints and/or risk tolerances that will trigger broad consideration of a potential need for intervention or modification of strategy?
<--- Score

10. Will the controls trigger any other risks?
<--- Score

11. Are events managed to resolution?
<--- Score

12. Which Holding companies solution is appropriate?

<--- Score

13. Are the key business and technology risks being managed?
<--- Score

14. To what extent does management recognize Holding companies as a tool to increase the results?
<--- Score

15. What were the criteria for evaluating a Holding companies pilot?
<--- Score

16. Why improve in the first place?
<--- Score

17. How do you measure risk?
<--- Score

18. Is supporting Holding companies documentation required?
<--- Score

19. What is the magnitude of the improvements?
<--- Score

20. Do vendor agreements bring new compliance risk ?
<--- Score

21. How are Holding companies risks managed?
<--- Score

22. How is continuous improvement applied to risk management?

<--- Score

23. Who are the Holding companies decision-makers?
<--- Score

24. In the past few months, what is the smallest change you have made that has had the biggest positive result? What was it about that small change that produced the large return?
<--- Score

25. For estimation problems, how do you develop an estimation statement?
<--- Score

26. What were the underlying assumptions on the cost-benefit analysis?
<--- Score

27. What are the implications of the one critical Holding companies decision 10 minutes, 10 months, and 10 years from now?
<--- Score

28. What risks do you need to manage?
<--- Score

29. Is the Holding companies risk managed?
<--- Score

30. Who should make the Holding companies decisions?
<--- Score

31. Is there any other Holding companies solution?
<--- Score

32. Are the most efficient solutions problem-specific?
<--- Score

33. What tools do you use once you have decided on a Holding companies strategy and more importantly how do you choose?
<--- Score

34. How can you better manage risk?
<--- Score

35. Can you integrate quality management and risk management?
<--- Score

36. How do you link measurement and risk?
<--- Score

37. Can you identify any significant risks or exposures to Holding companies third- parties (vendors, service providers, alliance partners etc) that concern you?
<--- Score

38. Is the measure of success for Holding companies understandable to a variety of people?
<--- Score

39. Is the Holding companies documentation thorough?
<--- Score

40. What area needs the greatest improvement?
<--- Score

41. What are your current levels and trends in key

measures or indicators of workforce and leader development?

<--- Score

42. Who will be using the results of the measurement activities?

<--- Score

43. What are the Holding companies security risks?

<--- Score

44. What strategies for Holding companies improvement are successful?

<--- Score

45. Is Holding companies documentation maintained?

<--- Score

46. Who manages Holding companies risk?

<--- Score

47. When you map the key players in your own work and the types/domains of relationships with them, which relationships do you find easy and which challenging, and why?

<--- Score

48. How do you go about comparing Holding companies approaches/solutions?

<--- Score

49. How is knowledge sharing about risk management improved?

<--- Score

50. What should a proof of concept or pilot

accomplish?
<--- Score

51. How do you define the solutions' scope?
<--- Score

52. What actually has to improve and by how much?
<--- Score

53. Can the solution be designed and implemented within an acceptable time period?
<--- Score

54. How do you decide how much to remunerate an employee?
<--- Score

55. How does your organization evaluate strategic Holding companies success?
<--- Score

56. Do you have the optimal project management team structure?
<--- Score

57. Are risk management tasks balanced centrally and locally?
<--- Score

58. Is risk periodically assessed?
<--- Score

59. What is the risk?
<--- Score

60. Is the Holding companies solution sustainable?

<--- Score

61. Where do the Holding companies decisions reside?
<--- Score

62. What can you do to improve?
<--- Score

63. Does a good decision guarantee a good outcome?
<--- Score

64. Would you develop a Holding companies Communication Strategy?
<--- Score

65. How significant is the improvement in the eyes of the end user?
<--- Score

66. What practices helps your organization to develop its capacity to recognize patterns?
<--- Score

67. Are decisions made in a timely manner?
<--- Score

68. Does the goal represent a desired result that can be measured?
<--- Score

69. Risk Identification: What are the possible risk events your organization faces in relation to Holding companies?
<--- Score

70. What needs improvement? Why?
<--- Score

71. Is there a high likelihood that any recommendations will achieve their intended results?
<--- Score

72. Risk factors: what are the characteristics of Holding companies that make it risky?
<--- Score

73. Who makes the Holding companies decisions in your organization?
<--- Score

74. What alternative responses are available to manage risk?
<--- Score

75. How do you improve your likelihood of success ?
<--- Score

76. What went well, what should change, what can improve?
<--- Score

77. How do you manage and improve your Holding companies work systems to deliver customer value and achieve organizational success and sustainability?
<--- Score

78. Who controls key decisions that will be made?
<--- Score

79. Risk events: what are the things that could go wrong?

<--- Score

80. What are the concrete Holding companies results?
<--- Score

81. What do you want to improve?
<--- Score

82. What resources are required for the improvement efforts?
<--- Score

83. What lessons, if any, from a pilot were incorporated into the design of the full-scale solution?
<--- Score

84. What tools were most useful during the improve phase?
<--- Score

85. What assumptions are made about the solution and approach?
<--- Score

86. Have you achieved Holding companies improvements?
<--- Score

87. How risky is your organization?
<--- Score

88. What to do with the results or outcomes of measurements?
<--- Score

89. How does the team improve its work?

<--- Score

90. Holding companies risk decisions: whose call Is It?
<--- Score

91. How scalable is your Holding companies solution?
<--- Score

92. What tools were used to evaluate the potential solutions?
<--- Score

93. Do you need to do a usability evaluation?
<--- Score

94. How will you know when its improved?
<--- Score

95. Are you assessing Holding companies and risk?
<--- Score

96. Are procedures documented for managing Holding companies risks?
<--- Score

97. What are the expected Holding companies results?
<--- Score

98. Do you combine technical expertise with business knowledge and Holding companies Key topics include lifecycles, development approaches, requirements and how to make a business case?
<--- Score

99. What is the team's contingency plan for potential problems occurring in implementation?

<--- Score

100. How can you improve Holding companies?
<--- Score

101. Where do you need Holding companies improvement?
<--- Score

102. Is the scope clearly documented?
<--- Score

103. What criteria will you use to assess your Holding companies risks?
<--- Score

104. Is the solution technically practical?
<--- Score

105. How do you manage Holding companies risk?
<--- Score

106. What current systems have to be understood and/or changed?
<--- Score

107. How do you keep improving Holding companies?
<--- Score

108. Do those selected for the Holding companies team have a good general understanding of what Holding companies is all about?
<--- Score

109. Are risk triggers captured?
<--- Score

110. What tools were used to tap into the creativity and encourage 'outside the box' thinking?
<--- Score

111. How do you measure improved Holding companies service perception, and satisfaction?
<--- Score

112. Which of the recognised risks out of all risks can be most likely transferred?
<--- Score

113. Who are the key stakeholders for the Holding companies evaluation?
<--- Score

114. If you could go back in time five years, what decision would you make differently? What is your best guess as to what decision you're making today you might regret five years from now?
<--- Score

115. How will you know that you have improved?
<--- Score

116. What improvements have been achieved?
<--- Score

117. For decision problems, how do you develop a decision statement?
<--- Score

118. How can skill-level changes improve Holding companies?
<--- Score

119. Who will be responsible for documenting the Holding companies requirements in detail?
<--- Score

120. How are policy decisions made and where?
<--- Score

121. How can the phases of Holding companies development be identified?
<--- Score

122. What is the Holding companies's sustainability risk?
<--- Score

123. Was a Holding companies charter developed?
<--- Score

124. Who do you report Holding companies results to?
<--- Score

125. What are the affordable Holding companies risks?
<--- Score

126. What Holding companies improvements can be made?
<--- Score

127. Are the risks fully understood, reasonable and manageable?
<--- Score

128. How do you mitigate Holding companies risk?
<--- Score

129. What is Holding companies risk?
<--- Score

130. At what point will vulnerability assessments be performed once Holding companies is put into production (e.g., ongoing Risk Management after implementation)?
<--- Score

131. Who manages supplier risk management in your organization?
<--- Score

Add up total points for this section:
_ _ _ _ _ = Total points for this section

Divided by: _ _ _ _ _ _ (number of statements answered) = _ _ _ _ _ _
Average score for this section

Transfer your score to the Holding companies Index at the beginning of the Self-Assessment.

CRITERION #6: CONTROL:

INTENT: Implement the practical solution. Maintain the performance and correct possible complications.

In my belief, the answer to this question is clearly defined:

5 Strongly Agree

4 Agree

3 Neutral

2 Disagree

1 Strongly Disagree

1. Is there an action plan in case of emergencies?
<--- Score

2. Who will be in control?
<--- Score

3. What is your plan to assess your security risks?
<--- Score

4. What is the control/monitoring plan?
<--- Score

5. Who has control over resources?
<--- Score

6. How will report readings be checked to effectively monitor performance?
<--- Score

7. Who sets the Holding companies standards?
<--- Score

8. What do you stand for--and what are you against?
<--- Score

9. What are the performance and scale of the Holding companies tools?
<--- Score

10. What are you attempting to measure/monitor?
<--- Score

11. How do you plan for the cost of succession?
<--- Score

12. What are the key elements of your Holding companies performance improvement system, including your evaluation, organizational learning, and innovation processes?
<--- Score

13. How do your controls stack up?
<--- Score

14. Is there a transfer of ownership and knowledge

to process owner and process team tasked with the
responsibilities.
<--- Score

15. Is there a recommended audit plan for routine
surveillance inspections of Holding companies's
gains?
<--- Score

16. Where do ideas that reach policy makers and
planners as proposals for Holding companies
strengthening and reform actually originate?
<--- Score

17. Does job training on the documented procedures
need to be part of the process team's education and
training?
<--- Score

18. Are the planned controls in place?
<--- Score

19. What are the critical parameters to watch?
<--- Score

20. How can you best use all of your knowledge
repositories to enhance learning and sharing?
<--- Score

21. Implementation Planning: is a pilot needed to test
the changes before a full roll out occurs?
<--- Score

22. Does the Holding companies performance meet
the customer's requirements?
<--- Score

23. Will your goals reflect your program budget?
<--- Score

24. What Holding companies standards are applicable?
<--- Score

25. What quality tools were useful in the control phase?
<--- Score

26. Are suggested corrective/restorative actions indicated on the response plan for known causes to problems that might surface?
<--- Score

27. Will any special training be provided for results interpretation?
<--- Score

28. Has the improved process and its steps been standardized?
<--- Score

29. How will the process owner verify improvement in present and future sigma levels, process capabilities?
<--- Score

30. Are the planned controls working?
<--- Score

31. Have new or revised work instructions resulted?
<--- Score

32. How do you monitor usage and cost?

<--- Score

33. Does the response plan contain a definite closed loop continual improvement scheme (e.g., plan-do-check-act)?
<--- Score

34. How do you encourage people to take control and responsibility?
<--- Score

35. Is a response plan in place for when the input, process, or output measures indicate an 'out-of-control' condition?
<--- Score

36. Is there a standardized process?
<--- Score

37. Do the Holding companies decisions you make today help people and the planet tomorrow?
<--- Score

38. How will new or emerging customer needs/requirements be checked/communicated to orient the process toward meeting the new specifications and continually reducing variation?
<--- Score

39. Who is going to spread your message?
<--- Score

40. In the case of a Holding companies project, the criteria for the audit derive from implementation objectives, an audit of a Holding companies project involves assessing whether the recommendations

outlined for implementation have been met, can you track that any Holding companies project is implemented as planned, and is it working?
<--- Score

41. Can you adapt and adjust to changing Holding companies situations?
<--- Score

42. You may have created your quality measures at a time when you lacked resources, technology wasn't up to the required standard, or low service levels were the industry norm. Have those circumstances changed?
<--- Score

43. How widespread is its use?
<--- Score

44. What is the standard for acceptable Holding companies performance?
<--- Score

45. Do you monitor the effectiveness of your Holding companies activities?
<--- Score

46. Do you monitor the Holding companies decisions made and fine tune them as they evolve?
<--- Score

47. How do senior leaders actions reflect a commitment to the organizations Holding companies values?
<--- Score

48. Are documented procedures clear and easy to follow for the operators?
<--- Score

49. What can you control?
<--- Score

50. Is there a control plan in place for sustaining improvements (short and long-term)?
<--- Score

51. Will existing staff require re-training, for example, to learn new business processes?
<--- Score

52. How will input, process, and output variables be checked to detect for sub-optimal conditions?
<--- Score

53. How will Holding companies decisions be made and monitored?
<--- Score

54. Are the Holding companies standards challenging?
<--- Score

55. How do you spread information?
<--- Score

56. Is reporting being used or needed?
<--- Score

57. Are new process steps, standards, and documentation ingrained into normal operations?
<--- Score

58. Do the viable solutions scale to future needs?
<--- Score

59. How do controls support value?
<--- Score

60. Is knowledge gained on process shared and institutionalized?
<--- Score

61. What do your reports reflect?
<--- Score

62. Is there a documented and implemented monitoring plan?
<--- Score

63. What other areas of the group might benefit from the Holding companies team's improvements, knowledge, and learning?
<--- Score

64. Does a troubleshooting guide exist or is it needed?
<--- Score

65. Will the team be available to assist members in planning investigations?
<--- Score

66. What key inputs and outputs are being measured on an ongoing basis?
<--- Score

67. How do you establish and deploy modified action plans if circumstances require a shift in plans and

rapid execution of new plans?

<--- Score

68. Are operating procedures consistent?

<--- Score

69. Are you measuring, monitoring and predicting Holding companies activities to optimize operations and profitability, and enhancing outcomes?

<--- Score

70. How will you measure your QA plan's effectiveness?

<--- Score

71. How will the day-to-day responsibilities for monitoring and continual improvement be transferred from the improvement team to the process owner?

<--- Score

72. How is change control managed?

<--- Score

73. Is a response plan established and deployed?

<--- Score

74. How do you select, collect, align, and integrate Holding companies data and information for tracking daily operations and overall organizational performance, including progress relative to strategic objectives and action plans?

<--- Score

75. Are pertinent alerts monitored, analyzed and distributed to appropriate personnel?

<--- Score

76. What should the next improvement project be that is related to Holding companies?
<--- Score

77. Are controls in place and consistently applied?
<--- Score

78. Are there documented procedures?
<--- Score

79. How is Holding companies project cost planned, managed, monitored?
<--- Score

80. Has the Holding companies value of standards been quantified?
<--- Score

81. How do you plan on providing proper recognition and disclosure of supporting companies?
<--- Score

82. Is the Holding companies test/monitoring cost justified?
<--- Score

83. What do you measure to verify effectiveness gains?
<--- Score

84. Is there a Holding companies Communication plan covering who needs to get what information when?
<--- Score

85. Against what alternative is success being measured?
<--- Score

86. What is the recommended frequency of auditing?
<--- Score

87. What is your theory of human motivation, and how does your compensation plan fit with that view?
<--- Score

88. Act/Adjust: What Do you Need to Do Differently?
<--- Score

89. What other systems, operations, processes, and infrastructures (hiring practices, staffing, training, incentives/rewards, metrics/dashboards/scorecards, etc.) need updates, additions, changes, or deletions in order to facilitate knowledge transfer and improvements?
<--- Score

90. Is there documentation that will support the successful operation of the improvement?
<--- Score

91. What are customers monitoring?
<--- Score

92. How likely is the current Holding companies plan to come in on schedule or on budget?
<--- Score

93. Who controls critical resources?
<--- Score

94. How might the group capture best practices and lessons learned so as to leverage improvements?
<--- Score

95. What should you measure to verify efficiency gains?
<--- Score

96. Who is the Holding companies process owner?
<--- Score

97. What is the best design framework for Holding companies organization now that, in a post industrial-age if the top-down, command and control model is no longer relevant?
<--- Score

98. Is new knowledge gained imbedded in the response plan?
<--- Score

99. How will the process owner and team be able to hold the gains?
<--- Score

100. Can support from partners be adjusted?
<--- Score

101. Does Holding companies appropriately measure and monitor risk?
<--- Score

Add up total points for this section:
_ _ _ _ _ = Total points for this section

Divided by: _ _ _ _ _ _ (number of

statements answered) = _____
Average score for this section

Transfer your score to the Holding
companies Index at the beginning of the
Self-Assessment.

CRITERION #7: SUSTAIN:

INTENT: Retain the benefits.

In my belief, the answer to this
question is clearly defined:

5 Strongly Agree

4 Agree

3 Neutral

2 Disagree

1 Strongly Disagree

1. If you find that you havent accomplished one of the
goals for one of the steps of the Holding companies
strategy, what will you do to fix it?
<--- Score

2. What projects are going on in the organization
today, and what resources are those projects using
from the resource pools?
<--- Score

3. What would have to be true for the option on the

table to be the best possible choice?
<--- Score

4. How much does Holding companies help?
<--- Score

5. Is it economical; do you have the time and money?
<--- Score

6. What does your signature ensure?
<--- Score

7. How will you motivate the stakeholders with the least vested interest?
<--- Score

8. What did you miss in the interview for the worst hire you ever made?
<--- Score

9. Did your employees make progress today?
<--- Score

10. How do you foster innovation?
<--- Score

11. What are you challenging?
<--- Score

12. How do you proactively clarify deliverables and Holding companies quality expectations?
<--- Score

13. What is it like to work for you?
<--- Score

14. What are the challenges?
<--- Score

15. What are you trying to prove to yourself, and how might it be hijacking your life and business success?
<--- Score

16. Whom among your colleagues do you trust, and for what?
<--- Score

17. Who, on the executive team or the board, has spoken to a customer recently?
<--- Score

18. How can you incorporate support to ensure safe and effective use of Holding companies into the services that you provide?
<--- Score

19. What happens at your organization when people fail?
<--- Score

20. What have been your experiences in defining long range Holding companies goals?
<--- Score

21. Who is responsible for Holding companies?
<--- Score

22. Is Holding companies realistic, or are you setting yourself up for failure?
<--- Score

23. If you had to leave your organization for a year

and the only communication you could have with employees/colleagues was a single paragraph, what would you write?

<--- Score

24. How do customers see your organization?

<--- Score

25. How do you accomplish your long range Holding companies goals?

<--- Score

26. How do you create buy-in?

<--- Score

27. Do you see more potential in people than they do in themselves?

<--- Score

28. Will there be any necessary staff changes (redundancies or new hires)?

<--- Score

29. How do senior leaders deploy your organizations vision and values through your leadership system, to the workforce, to key suppliers and partners, and to customers and other stakeholders, as appropriate?

<--- Score

30. Is maximizing Holding companies protection the same as minimizing Holding companies loss?

<--- Score

31. What will be the consequences to the stakeholder (financial, reputation etc) if Holding companies does not go ahead or fails to deliver the objectives?

<--- Score

32. Are you satisfied with your current role? If not, what is missing from it?
<--- Score

33. How will you ensure you get what you expected?
<--- Score

34. How do you foster the skills, knowledge, talents, attributes, and characteristics you want to have?
<--- Score

35. Do you know who is a friend or a foe?
<--- Score

36. Are new benefits received and understood?
<--- Score

37. What is the kind of project structure that would be appropriate for your Holding companies project, should it be formal and complex, or can it be less formal and relatively simple?
<--- Score

38. How do you manage Holding companies Knowledge Management (KM)?
<--- Score

39. How can you become the company that would put you out of business?
<--- Score

40. How do you determine the key elements that affect Holding companies workforce satisfaction, how are these elements determined for different workforce

groups and segments?

<--- Score

41. Is a Holding companies team work effort in place?

<--- Score

42. How do you track customer value, profitability or financial return, organizational success, and sustainability?

<--- Score

43. How will you insure seamless interoperability of Holding companies moving forward?

<--- Score

44. How do you cross-sell and up-sell your Holding companies success?

<--- Score

45. Do Holding companies rules make a reasonable demand on a users capabilities?

<--- Score

46. Why should you adopt a Holding companies framework?

<--- Score

47. How likely is it that a customer would recommend your company to a friend or colleague?

<--- Score

48. Is the Holding companies organization completing tasks effectively and efficiently?

<--- Score

49. How can you negotiate Holding companies

successfully with a stubborn boss, an irate client, or a deceitful coworker?

<--- Score

50. Why not do Holding companies?

<--- Score

51. Is a Holding companies breakthrough on the horizon?

<--- Score

52. Who else should you help?

<--- Score

53. Who do you think the world wants your organization to be?

<--- Score

54. How do you keep the momentum going?

<--- Score

55. If your customer were your grandmother, would you tell her to buy what you're selling?

<--- Score

56. What are strategies for increasing support and reducing opposition?

<--- Score

57. What potential megatrends could make your business model obsolete?

<--- Score

58. In a project to restructure Holding companies outcomes, which stakeholders would you involve?

<--- Score

59. Can you maintain your growth without detracting from the factors that have contributed to your success?
<--- Score

60. What would you recommend your friend do if he/she were facing this dilemma?
<--- Score

61. Have new benefits been realized?
<--- Score

62. Do you have enough freaky customers in your portfolio pushing you to the limit day in and day out?
<--- Score

63. How do you deal with Holding companies changes?
<--- Score

64. Are you maintaining a past–present–future perspective throughout the Holding companies discussion?
<--- Score

65. Why is Holding companies important for you now?
<--- Score

66. To whom do you add value?
<--- Score

67. What are the top 3 things at the forefront of your Holding companies agendas for the next 3 years?
<--- Score

68. Is corporate governance different for organization holding companies?

<--- Score

69. Do you have past Holding companies successes?
<--- Score

70. What knowledge, skills and characteristics mark a good Holding companies project manager?
<--- Score

71. What are the rules and assumptions your industry operates under? What if the opposite were true?
<--- Score

72. How is implementation research currently incorporated into each of your goals?
<--- Score

73. Can the schedule be done in the given time?
<--- Score

74. Why is it important to have senior management support for a Holding companies project?
<--- Score

75. Who is responsible for ensuring appropriate resources (time, people and money) are allocated to Holding companies?
<--- Score

76. Are your responses positive or negative?
<--- Score

77. What threat is Holding companies addressing?
<--- Score

78. If you do not follow, then how to lead?
<--- Score

79. If your company went out of business tomorrow, would anyone who doesn't get a paycheck here care?
<--- Score

80. How do you stay inspired?
<--- Score

81. What is effective Holding companies?
<--- Score

82. Who will manage the integration of tools?
<--- Score

83. What role does communication play in the success or failure of a Holding companies project?
<--- Score

84. What is your formula for success in Holding companies ?
<--- Score

85. Who do you want your customers to become?
<--- Score

86. If you were responsible for initiating and implementing major changes in your organization, what steps might you take to ensure acceptance of those changes?
<--- Score

87. Is your basic point _____ or _____?
<--- Score

88. Who is the main stakeholder, with ultimate responsibility for driving Holding companies forward?
<--- Score

89. Are you / should you be revolutionary or evolutionary?
<--- Score

90. What counts that you are not counting?
<--- Score

91. How do you provide a safe environment -physically and emotionally?
<--- Score

92. What business benefits will Holding companies goals deliver if achieved?
<--- Score

93. Instead of going to current contacts for new ideas, what if you reconnected with dormant contacts-- the people you used to know? If you were going reactivate a dormant tie, who would it be?
<--- Score

94. What is the overall talent health of your organization as a whole at senior levels, and for each organization reporting to a member of the Senior Leadership Team?
<--- Score

95. What is a feasible sequencing of reform initiatives over time?
<--- Score

96. Are you making progress, and are you making progress as Holding companies leaders?
<--- Score

97. What is the source of the strategies for Holding companies strengthening and reform?
<--- Score

98. Are you using a design thinking approach and integrating Innovation, Holding companies Experience, and Brand Value?
<--- Score

99. Who are the key stakeholders?
<--- Score

100. Do you say no to customers for no reason?
<--- Score

101. How do you go about securing Holding companies?
<--- Score

102. Think of your Holding companies project, what are the main functions?
<--- Score

103. What are your personal philosophies regarding Holding companies and how do they influence your work?
<--- Score

104. Are the criteria for selecting recommendations stated?
<--- Score

105. What is the recommended frequency of auditing?
<--- Score

106. What is the purpose of Holding companies in relation to the mission?
<--- Score

107. Is your strategy driving your strategy? Or is the way in which you allocate resources driving your strategy?
<--- Score

108. Are assumptions made in Holding companies stated explicitly?
<--- Score

109. Who will determine interim and final deadlines?
<--- Score

110. If you had to rebuild your organization without any traditional competitive advantages (i.e., no killer technology, promising research, innovative product/ service delivery model, etcetera), how would your people have to approach their work and collaborate together in order to create the necessary conditions for success?
<--- Score

111. What trophy do you want on your mantle?
<--- Score

112. What are your most important goals for the strategic Holding companies objectives?
<--- Score

113. How do you engage the workforce, in addition to

satisfying them?
<--- Score

114. Are you relevant? Will you be relevant five years from now? Ten?
<--- Score

115. If no one would ever find out about your accomplishments, how would you lead differently?
<--- Score

116. Who is responsible for errors?
<--- Score

117. What are the usability implications of Holding companies actions?
<--- Score

118. What do we do when new problems arise?
<--- Score

119. What are the barriers to increased Holding companies production?
<--- Score

120. Have benefits been optimized with all key stakeholders?
<--- Score

121. Will it be accepted by users?
<--- Score

122. Are all key stakeholders present at all Structured Walkthroughs?
<--- Score

123. What are the gaps in your knowledge and experience?
<--- Score

124. What may be the consequences for the performance of an organization if all stakeholders are not consulted regarding Holding companies?
<--- Score

125. What is the overall business strategy?
<--- Score

126. Is Holding companies dependent on the successful delivery of a current project?
<--- Score

127. Who will provide the final approval of Holding companies deliverables?
<--- Score

128. Has implementation been effective in reaching specified objectives so far?
<--- Score

129. How do you set Holding companies stretch targets and how do you get people to not only participate in setting these stretch targets but also that they strive to achieve these?
<--- Score

130. What is the craziest thing you can do?
<--- Score

131. Marketing budgets are tighter, consumers are more skeptical, and social media has changed forever the way we talk about Holding companies, how do

you gain traction?
<--- Score

132. How do you govern and fulfill your societal responsibilities?
<--- Score

133. Do you have the right capabilities and capacities?
<--- Score

134. What is your competitive advantage?
<--- Score

135. What are the long-term Holding companies goals?
<--- Score

136. Is there any reason to believe the opposite of my current belief?
<--- Score

137. Whose voice (department, ethnic group, women, older workers, etc) might you have missed hearing from in your company, and how might you amplify this voice to create positive momentum for your business?
<--- Score

138. What Holding companies modifications can you make work for you?
<--- Score

139. Are you changing as fast as the world around you?
<--- Score

140. What new services of functionality will be implemented next with Holding companies ?
<--- Score

141. How do you know if you are successful?
<--- Score

142. Who have you, as a company, historically been when you've been at your best?
<--- Score

143. What have you done to protect your business from competitive encroachment?
<--- Score

144. Were lessons learned captured and communicated?
<--- Score

145. If there were zero limitations, what would you do differently?
<--- Score

146. How do you transition from the baseline to the target?
<--- Score

147. What happens if you do not have enough funding?
<--- Score

148. What goals did you miss?
<--- Score

149. Is there a work around that you can use?
<--- Score

150. Do you have the right people on the bus?
<--- Score

151. Are there any activities that you can take off your to do list?
<--- Score

152. What information is critical to your organization that your executives are ignoring?
<--- Score

153. How much contingency will be available in the budget?
<--- Score

154. What you are going to do to affect the numbers?
<--- Score

155. What should you stop doing?
<--- Score

156. Do you have an implicit bias for capital investments over people investments?
<--- Score

157. Are you paying enough attention to the partners your company depends on to succeed?
<--- Score

158. Which Holding companies goals are the most important?
<--- Score

159. What one word do you want to own in the minds of your customers, employees, and partners?

<--- Score

160. Why will customers want to buy your organizations products/services?
<--- Score

161. How do you listen to customers to obtain actionable information?
<--- Score

162. What relationships among Holding companies trends do you perceive?
<--- Score

163. What is your BATNA (best alternative to a negotiated agreement)?
<--- Score

164. How do you keep records, of what?
<--- Score

165. In the past year, what have you done (or could you have done) to increase the accurate perception of your company/brand as ethical and honest?
<--- Score

166. Do you think Holding companies accomplishes the goals you expect it to accomplish?
<--- Score

167. Which models, tools and techniques are necessary?
<--- Score

168. When information truly is ubiquitous, when reach and connectivity are completely global, when

computing resources are infinite, and when a whole new set of impossibilities are not only possible, but happening, what will that do to your business?
<--- Score

169. How will you know that the Holding companies project has been successful?
<--- Score

170. What is the big Holding companies idea?
<--- Score

171. Do you know what you are doing? And who do you call if you don't?
<--- Score

172. How important is Holding companies to the user organizations mission?
<--- Score

173. Do you feel that more should be done in the Holding companies area?
<--- Score

174. What are specific Holding companies rules to follow?
<--- Score

175. Can you break it down?
<--- Score

176. What must you excel at?
<--- Score

177. Who uses your product in ways you never expected?

<--- Score

178. What are the business goals Holding companies is aiming to achieve?
<--- Score

179. Do you think you know, or do you know you know ?
<--- Score

180. At what moment would you think; Will I get fired?
<--- Score

181. How do you maintain Holding companies's Integrity?
<--- Score

182. What is something you believe that nearly no one agrees with you on?
<--- Score

183. What trouble can you get into?
<--- Score

184. Which functions and people interact with the supplier and or customer?
<--- Score

185. In retrospect, of the projects that you pulled the plug on, what percent do you wish had been allowed to keep going, and what percent do you wish had ended earlier?
<--- Score

186. What stupid rule would you most like to kill?
<--- Score

187. What is the range of capabilities?
<--- Score

188. What is the funding source for this project?
<--- Score

189. What are the success criteria that will indicate that Holding companies objectives have been met and the benefits delivered?
<--- Score

190. What are internal and external Holding companies relations?
<--- Score

191. What is the estimated value of the project?
<--- Score

192. Who will be responsible for deciding whether Holding companies goes ahead or not after the initial investigations?
<--- Score

193. What are current Holding companies paradigms?
<--- Score

194. What are the essentials of internal Holding companies management?
<--- Score

195. Who is on the team?
<--- Score

196. What Holding companies skills are most important?

<--- Score

197. Who do we want your customers to become?
<--- Score

198. Which individuals, teams or departments will be involved in Holding companies?
<--- Score

199. What are the potential basics of Holding companies fraud?
<--- Score

200. Is there any existing Holding companies governance structure?
<--- Score

201. What management system can you use to leverage the Holding companies experience, ideas, and concerns of the people closest to the work to be done?
<--- Score

202. If you got fired and a new hire took your place, what would she do different?
<--- Score

203. What are the key enablers to make this Holding companies move?
<--- Score

204. Who are four people whose careers you have enhanced?
<--- Score

205. Is the impact that Holding companies has

shown?
<--- Score

206. What was the last experiment you ran?
<--- Score

207. Political -is anyone trying to undermine this project?
<--- Score

208. Can you do all this work?
<--- Score

209. Operational - will it work?
<--- Score

210. How long will it take to change?
<--- Score

211. How do you lead with Holding companies in mind?
<--- Score

212. What unique value proposition (UVP) do you offer?
<--- Score

213. What is your Holding companies strategy?
<--- Score

214. How does Holding companies integrate with other stakeholder initiatives?
<--- Score

215. Why do and why don't your customers like your organization?

<--- Score

Add up total points for this section:
_ _ _ _ _ = Total points for this section

Divided by: _ _ _ _ _ _ (number of
statements answered) = _ _ _ _ _ _
Average score for this section

Transfer your score to the Holding
companies Index at the beginning of the
Self-Assessment.

Holding Companies and Managing Projects, Criteria for Project Managers:

1.0 Initiating Process Group: Holding Companies

1. Were resources available as planned?

2. At which stage, in a typical Holding Companies project do stake holders have maximum influence?

3. Realistic - are the desired results expressed in a way that the team will be motivated and believe that the required level of involvement will be obtained?

4. Are the changes in your Holding Companies project being formally requested, analyzed, and approved by the appropriate decision makers?

5. How will it affect me?

6. Who are the Holding Companies project stakeholders?

7. Who is behind the Holding Companies project?

8. Who is performing the work of the Holding Companies project?

9. Who does what?

10. Are you properly tracking the progress of the Holding Companies project and communicating the status to stakeholders?

11. What are the inputs required to produce the deliverables?

12. What is the NEXT thing to do?

13. Will the Holding Companies project meet the client requirements, and will it achieve the business success criteria that justified doing the Holding Companies project in the first place?

14. What were things that you did very well and want to do the same again on the next Holding Companies project?

15. Do you know all the stakeholders impacted by the Holding Companies project and what needs are?

16. Did the Holding Companies project team have the right skills?

17. What are the required resources?

18. Which of six sigmas dmaic phases focuses on the measurement of internal process that affect factors that are critical to quality?

19. How will you do it?

20. Who is funding the Holding Companies project?

1.1 Project Charter: Holding Companies

21. Major high-level milestone targets: what events measure progress?

22. Why executive support?

23. What material?

24. What metrics could you look at?

25. Does the Holding Companies project need to consider any special capacity or capability issues?

26. Who is the sponsor?

27. Why is it important?

28. How will you learn more about the process or system you are trying to improve?

29. What barriers do you predict to your success?

30. Who will take notes, document decisions?

31. Did your Holding Companies project ask for this?

32. How will you know a change is an improvement?

33. What are the assumptions?

34. Are you building in-house ?

35. Why use a Holding Companies project charter?

36. Holding Companies project deliverables: what is the Holding Companies project going to produce?

37. Why do you need to manage scope?

38. Who ise input and support will this Holding Companies project require?

39. Why Outsource?

1.2 Stakeholder Register: Holding Companies

40. How big is the gap?

41. What opportunities exist to provide communications?

42. Who are the stakeholders?

43. How much influence do they have on the Holding Companies project?

44. What is the power of the stakeholder?

45. How will reports be created?

46. What are the major Holding Companies project milestones requiring communications or providing communications opportunities?

47. What & Why?

48. Who is managing stakeholder engagement?

49. How should employers make voices heard?

50. Is your organization ready for change?

51. Who wants to talk about Security?

1.3 Stakeholder Analysis Matrix: Holding Companies

52. Why do you need to manage Holding Companies project Risk?

53. Seasonality, weather effects?

54. What makes a person a stakeholder?

55. Market demand?

56. How do they affect the Holding Companies project and its outcomes?

57. Vital contracts and partners?

58. What advantages do your organizations stakeholders have?

59. What unique or lowest-cost resources does the Holding Companies project have access to?

60. Experience, knowledge, data?

61. Effects on core activities, distraction?

62. Sustaining internal capabilities?

63. What do people from other organizations see as your strengths?

64. Who will be affected by the work?

65. Information and research?

66. What is the range you need to look at?

67. What organizational arrangements are planned to ensure the Holding Companies project achieves its social development outcomes?

68. Who has the power to influence the outcomes of the work?

69. How do rules, behaviors affect stakes?

70. Who holds positions of responsibility in interested organizations?

71. What could your organization improve?

2.0 Planning Process Group: Holding Companies

72. How will users learn how to use the deliverables?

73. You did your readings, yes?

74. How should needs be met?

75. To what extent has a PMO contributed to raising the quality of the design of the Holding Companies project?

76. What will you do to minimize the impact should a risk event occur?

77. If a risk event occurs, what will you do?

78. To what extent has the intervention strategy been adapted to the areas of intervention in which it is being implemented?

79. How well did the chosen processes fit the needs of the Holding Companies project?

80. What type of estimation method are you using?

81. To what extent do the intervention objectives and strategies of the Holding Companies project respond to your organizations plans?

82. What should you do next?

83. What input will you be required to provide the Holding Companies project team?

84. Are there efficient coordination mechanisms to avoid overloading the counterparts, participating stakeholders?

85. Does the program have follow-up mechanisms (to verify the quality of the products, punctuality of delivery, etc.) to measure progress in the achievement of the envisaged results?

86. Are the follow-up indicators relevant and do they meet the quality needed to measure the outputs and outcomes of the Holding Companies project?

87. In what way has the program contributed towards the issue culture and development included on the public agenda?

88. Just how important is your work to the overall success of the Holding Companies project?

89. What factors are contributing to progress or delay in the achievement of products and results?

90. How are the principles of aid effectiveness (ownership, alignment, management for development results and mutual responsibility) being applied in the Holding Companies project?

2.1 Project Management Plan: Holding Companies

91. Does the selected plan protect privacy?

92. What are the deliverables?

93. What did not work so well?

94. Are cost risk analysis methods applied to develop contingencies for the estimated total Holding Companies project costs?

95. Is the budget realistic?

96. Is there an incremental analysis/cost effectiveness analysis of proposed mitigation features based on an approved method and using an accepted model?

97. What is the justification?

98. What are the constraints?

99. What are the known stakeholder requirements?

100. Do the proposed changes from the Holding Companies project include any significant risks to safety?

101. What would you do differently what did not work?

102. Was the peer (technical) review of the cost

estimates duly coordinated with the cost estimate center of expertise and addressed in the review documentation and certification?

103. Are the existing and future without-plan conditions reasonable and appropriate?

104. How do you organize the costs in the Holding Companies project management plan?

105. What goes into your Holding Companies project Charter?

106. Will you add a schedule and diagram?

107. What should you drop in order to add something new?

108. What is risk management?

109. Are there non-structural buyout or relocation recommendations?

2.2 Scope Management Plan: Holding Companies

110. What work performance data will be captured?

111. What are the risks that could significantly affect the budget of the Holding Companies project?

112. Is there a requirements change management processes in place?

113. Cost / benefit analysis?

114. What is your organizations history in doing similar activities?

115. Are the results of quality assurance reviews provided to affected groups & individuals?

116. Is there any form of automated support for Issues Management?

117. Are issues raised, assessed, actioned, and resolved in a timely and efficient manner?

118. Are milestone deliverables effectively tracked and compared to Holding Companies project plan?

119. Are software metrics formally captured, analyzed and used as a basis for other Holding Companies project estimates?

120. Has a Holding Companies project

Communications Plan been developed?

121. Quality standards - are controls in place to ensure that the work was not only completed and also completed to meet specific standards?

122. Can each item be appropriately scheduled?

123. Is the quality assurance team identified?

124. Is there a formal set of procedures supporting Issues Management?

125. Are tasks tracked by hours?

126. Are meeting objectives identified for each meeting?

2.3 Requirements Management Plan: Holding Companies

127. How do you know that you have done this right?

128. How knowledgeable is the team in the proposed application area?

129. Is there formal agreement on who has authority to request a change in requirements?

130. How will you communicate scheduled tasks to other team members?

131. The wbs is developed as part of a joint planning session. and how do you know that youhave done this right?

132. Did you avoid subjective, flowery or non-specific statements?

133. Do you know which stakeholders will participate in the requirements effort?

134. Is it new or replacing an existing business system or process?

135. Is the change control process documented?

136. Does the Holding Companies project have a Change Control process?

137. How will requirements be managed?

138. How will the information be distributed?

139. What is a problem?

140. Who will finally present the work or product(s) for acceptance?

141. Do you have an appropriate arrangement for meetings?

142. What cost metrics will be used?

143. Will you document changes to requirements?

144. How detailed should the Holding Companies project get?

145. Are actual resources expenditures versus planned expenditures acceptable?

146. Business analysis scope?

2.4 Requirements Documentation: Holding Companies

147. What is a show stopper in the requirements?

148. How can you document system requirements?

149. What are the acceptance criteria?

150. How much testing do you need to do to prove that your system is safe?

151. Can the requirement be changed without a large impact on other requirements?

152. How much does requirements engineering cost?

153. What facilities must be supported by the system?

154. Are all functions required by the customer included?

155. Is the requirement properly understood?

156. What is effective documentation?

157. How will the proposed Holding Companies project help?

158. What are the attributes of a customer?

159. What marketing channels do you want to use: e-mail, letter or sms?

160. How do you get the user to tell you what they want?

161. What variations exist for a process?

162. What kind of entity is a problem ?

163. What are current process problems?

164. Is new technology needed?

165. Is the requirement realistically testable?

166. If applicable; are there issues linked with the fact that this is an offshore Holding Companies project?

2.5 Requirements Traceability Matrix: Holding Companies

167. Do you have a clear understanding of all subcontracts in place?

168. What percentage of Holding Companies projects are producing traceability matrices between requirements and other work products?

169. Describe the process for approving requirements so they can be added to the traceability matrix and Holding Companies project work can be performed. Will the Holding Companies project requirements become approved in writing?

170. What are the chronologies, contingencies, consequences, criteria?

171. Is there a requirements traceability process in place?

172. What is the WBS?

173. Will you use a Requirements Traceability Matrix?

174. How will it affect the stakeholders personally in career?

175. How small is small enough?

176. How do you manage scope?

177. Why use a WBS?

178. Why do you manage scope?

2.6 Project Scope Statement: Holding Companies

179. Is there a baseline plan against which to measure progress?

180. Are there completion/verification criteria defined for each task producing an output?

181. Has a method and process for requirement tracking been developed?

182. Are there specific processes you will use to evaluate and approve/reject changes?

183. Will this process be communicated to the customer and Holding Companies project team?

184. Will an issue form be in use?

185. Is your organization structure appropriate for the Holding Companies projects size and complexity?

186. Elements that deal with providing the detail?

187. What are the major deliverables of the Holding Companies project?

188. Is there an information system for the Holding Companies project?

189. Is the change control process documented and on file?

190. Are there issues that could affect the existing requirements for the result, service, or product if the scope changes?

191. Will there be a Change Control Process in place?

192. What are the possible consequences should a risk come to occur?

193. Is an issue management process documented and filed?

194. Holding Companies project lead, team lead, solution architect?

195. What is change?

196. Relevant - ask yourself can you get there; why are you doing this Holding Companies project?

197. What are the defined meeting materials?

2.7 Assumption and Constraint Log: Holding Companies

198. Is staff trained on the software technologies that are being used on the Holding Companies project?

199. Does the plan conform to standards?

200. What to do at recovery?

201. How many Holding Companies project staff does this specific process affect?

202. Would known impacts serve as impediments?

203. Is this model reasonable?

204. Are there ways to reduce the time it takes to get something approved?

205. Is the amount of effort justified by the anticipated value of forming a new process?

206. Does the Holding Companies project have a formal Holding Companies project Plan?

207. What strengths do you have?

208. Has the approach and development strategy of the Holding Companies project been defined, documented and accepted by the appropriate stakeholders?

209. Contradictory information between different documents?

210. What if failure during recovery?

211. Has a Holding Companies project Communications Plan been developed?

212. How relevant is this attribute to this Holding Companies project or audit?

213. Is the steering committee active in Holding Companies project oversight?

214. Is this process still needed?

215. What worked well?

216. Were the system requirements formally reviewed prior to initiating the design phase?

2.8 Work Breakdown Structure: Holding Companies

217. Is it still viable?

218. When would you develop a Work Breakdown Structure?

219. Who has to do it?

220. Do you need another level?

221. Is the work breakdown structure (wbs) defined and is the scope of the Holding Companies project clear with assigned deliverable owners?

222. When do you stop?

223. Why would you develop a Work Breakdown Structure?

224. When does it have to be done?

225. What is the probability of completing the Holding Companies project in less that xx days?

226. How much detail?

227. How big is a work-package?

228. What is the probability that the Holding Companies project duration will exceed xx weeks?

229. How far down?

230. How many levels?

231. Why is it useful?

232. Where does it take place?

2.9 WBS Dictionary: Holding Companies

233. Are data elements (BCWS, BCWP, and ACWP) progressively summarized from the detail level to the contract level through the CWBS?

234. Are the contractors estimates of costs at completion reconcilable with cost data reported to us?

235. Does the contractor use objective results, design reviews and tests to trace schedule performance?

236. Does the accounting system provide a basis for auditing records of direct costs chargeable to the contract?

237. Contemplated overhead expenditure for each period based on the best information currently available?

238. Are indirect costs accumulated for comparison with the corresponding budgets?

239. Are estimates developed by Holding Companies project personnel coordinated with the already stated responsible for overall management to determine whether required resources will be available according to revised planning?

240. What went right?

241. Is cost and schedule performance measurement done in a consistent, systematic manner?

242. Are detailed work packages planned as far in advance as practicable?

243. The anticipated business volume?

244. Knowledgeable Holding Companies projections of future performance?

245. Are the bases and rates for allocating costs from each indirect pool to commercial work consistent with the already stated used to allocate corresponding costs to Government contracts?

246. Does the cost accumulation system provide for summarization of indirect costs from the point of allocation to the contract total?

247. Are the procedures for identifying indirect costs to incurring organizations, indirect cost pools, and allocating the costs from the pools to the contracts formally documented?

248. Does the scheduling system identify in a timely manner the status of work?

249. What is wrong with this Holding Companies project?

250. Does the contractors system include procedures for measuring the performance of critical subcontractors?

251. Are the requirements for all items of overhead

established by rational, traceable processes?

252. Are data elements reconcilable between internal summary reports and reports forwarded to us?

2.10 Schedule Management Plan: Holding Companies

253. Have the key elements of a coherent Holding Companies project management strategy been established?

254. Is the critical path valid?

255. Are action items captured and managed?

256. Are staff skills known and available for each task?

257. Are the processes for status updates and maintenance defined?

258. Was your organizations estimating methodology being used and followed?

259. Are right task and resource calendars used in the IMS?

260. Time for overtime?

261. Are cause and effect determined for risks when they occur?

262. Are all resource assumptions documented?

263. Is there an excessive and invalid use of task constraints and relationships of leads/lags?

264. Staffing Requirements?

265. Is the assigned Holding Companies project manager a PMP (Certified Holding Companies project manager) and experienced?

266. Is stakeholder involvement adequate?

267. Are all activities captured and do they address all approved work scope in the Holding Companies project baseline?

268. Are enough systems & user personnel assigned to the Holding Companies project?

269. Are estimating assumptions and constraints captured?

270. Pareto diagrams, statistical sampling, flow charting or trend analysis used quality monitoring?

271. Has the scope management document been updated and distributed to help prevent scope creep?

2.11 Activity List: Holding Companies

272. Are the required resources available or need to be acquired?

273. How should ongoing costs be monitored to try to keep the Holding Companies project within budget?

274. What are the critical bottleneck activities?

275. How do you determine the late start (LS) for each activity?

276. In what sequence?

277. How difficult will it be to do specific activities on this Holding Companies project?

278. What went well?

279. Is infrastructure setup part of your Holding Companies project?

280. What are you counting on?

281. What is the LF and LS for each activity?

282. Can you determine the activity that must finish, before this activity can start?

283. What is the total time required to complete the Holding Companies project if no delays occur?

284. How will it be performed?

285. When will the work be performed?

286. What will be performed?

287. What went wrong?

288. Is there anything planned that does not need to be here?

2.12 Activity Attributes: Holding Companies

289. Resource is assigned to?

290. How else could the items be grouped?

291. How difficult will it be to complete specific activities on this Holding Companies project?

292. Resources to accomplish the work?

293. Has management defined a definite timeframe for the turnaround or Holding Companies project window?

294. How difficult will it be to do specific activities on this Holding Companies project?

295. Have constraints been applied to the start and finish milestones for the phases?

296. How much activity detail is required?

297. Have you identified the Activity Leveling Priority code value on each activity?

298. What conclusions/generalizations can you draw from this?

299. How many days do you need to complete the work scope with a limit of X number of resources?

300. Which method produces the more accurate cost assignment?

301. Where else does it apply?

302. What is missing?

303. How do you manage time?

304. Why?

2.13 Milestone List: Holding Companies

305. New USPs?

306. Obstacles faced?

307. Which path is the critical path?

308. Sustainable financial backing?

309. How late can each activity be finished and started?

310. What are your competitors vulnerabilities?

311. What date will the task finish?

312. Describe the concept of the technology, product or service that will be or has been developed. How will it be used?

313. Global influences?

314. Can you derive how soon can the whole Holding Companies project finish?

315. How late can the activity start?

316. Timescales, deadlines and pressures?

317. Level of the Innovation?

318. What is the market for your technology, product or service?

319. Do you foresee any technical risks or developmental challenges?

2.14 Network Diagram: Holding Companies

320. Exercise: what is the probability that the Holding Companies project duration will exceed xx weeks?

321. What is the lowest cost to complete this Holding Companies project in xx weeks?

322. What job or jobs could run concurrently?

323. What are the Key Success Factors?

324. What are the Major Administrative Issues?

325. Can you calculate the confidence level?

326. Are you on time?

327. What are the tools?

328. Where do schedules come from?

329. Are the gantt chart and/or network diagram updated periodically and used to assess the overall Holding Companies project timetable?

330. What is the completion time?

331. What job or jobs follow it?

332. Planning: who, how long, what to do?

333. If the Holding Companies project network diagram cannot change and you have extra personnel resources, what is the BEST thing to do?

334. What to do and When?

335. What can be done concurrently?

336. How difficult will it be to do specific activities on this Holding Companies project?

337. Where do you schedule uncertainty time?

338. What must be completed before an activity can be started?

339. Which type of network diagram allows you to depict four types of dependencies?

2.15 Activity Resource Requirements: Holding Companies

340. What are constraints that you might find during the Human Resource Planning process?

341. Which logical relationship does the PDM use most often?

342. Do you use tools like decomposition and rolling-wave planning to produce the activity list and other outputs?

343. When does monitoring begin?

344. How do you handle petty cash?

345. What is the Work Plan Standard?

346. Anything else?

347. Other support in specific areas?

348. How many signatures do you require on a check and does this match what is in your policy and procedures?

349. Organizational Applicability?

350. Are there unresolved issues that need to be addressed?

351. Why do you do that?

2.16 Resource Breakdown Structure: Holding Companies

352. What is the purpose of assigning and documenting responsibility?

353. Who needs what information?

354. How difficult will it be to do specific activities on this Holding Companies project?

355. Is predictive resource analysis being done?

356. The list could probably go on, but, the thing that you would most like to know is, How long & How much?

357. What is the difference between % Complete and % work?

358. Why time management?

359. What is the primary purpose of the human resource plan?

360. What defines a successful Holding Companies project?

361. How should the information be delivered?

362. Why is this important?

363. Changes based on input from stakeholders?

364. Which resources should be in the resource pool?

365. Any changes from stakeholders?

366. What is the number one predictor of a groups productivity?

367. Who is allowed to perform which functions?

368. What is Holding Companies project communication management?

369. Who delivers the information?

2.17 Activity Duration Estimates: Holding Companies

370. Are inspections completed to determine if the results comply with the requirements?

371. Why is activity definition the first process involved in Holding Companies project time management?

372. How is the Holding Companies project doing?

373. Are activity dependencies identified?

374. Is action taken to increase the effectiveness and efficiency of Holding Companies projects?

375. How does Holding Companies project management relate to other disciplines?

376. Is a Holding Companies project charter created once a Holding Companies project is formally recognized?

377. What type of contract was used and why?

378. Can they use the already stated?

379. Is risk identification completed regularly throughout the Holding Companies project?

380. Do scope statements include the Holding Companies project objectives and expected

deliverables?

381. What type of activity sequencing method is required for corresponding activities?

382. Did anything besides luck make a difference between success and failure?

383. What is the duration of the critical path for this Holding Companies project?

384. Are training needs identified when resources do not have the required skills to complete Holding Companies project activities?

385. Consider the changes in the job market for information technology workers. How does the job market and current state of the economy affect human resource management?

386. Based on , if you need to shorten the duration of the Holding Companies project, what activity would you try to shorten?

387. Mass, power, cost ... why not time?

388. After how many days will the lease cost be the same as the purchase cost for the equipment?

389. Do they make sense?

2.18 Duration Estimating Worksheet: Holding Companies

390. What is the total time required to complete the Holding Companies project if no delays occur?

391. What is an Average Holding Companies project?

392. Why estimate time and cost?

393. What work will be included in the Holding Companies project?

394. For other activities, how much delay can be tolerated?

395. Done before proceeding with this activity or what can be done concurrently?

396. Is a construction detail attached (to aid in explanation)?

397. Do any colleagues have experience with your organization and/or RFPs?

398. Why estimate costs?

399. What is cost and Holding Companies project cost management?

400. How should ongoing costs be monitored to try to keep the Holding Companies project within budget?

401. What questions do you have?

402. What utility impacts are there?

403. When does your organization expect to be able to complete it?

404. Define the work as completely as possible. What work will be included in the Holding Companies project?

405. When do the individual activities need to start and finish?

406. Can the Holding Companies project be constructed as planned?

407. What is next?

408. When, then?

2.19 Project Schedule: Holding Companies

409. What is the purpose of a Holding Companies project schedule?

410. Why or why not?

411. Verify that the update is accurate. Are all remaining durations correct?

412. Master Holding Companies project schedule?

413. Holding Companies project work estimates Who is managing the work estimate quality of work tasks in the Holding Companies project schedule?

414. How do you manage Holding Companies project Risk?

415. Should you have a test for each code module?

416. How much slack is available in the Holding Companies project?

417. How can you minimize or control changes to Holding Companies project schedules?

418. Are activities connected because logic dictates the order in which others occur?

419. What is Holding Companies project management?

420. Are quality inspections and review activities listed in the Holding Companies project schedule(s)?

421. How can you address that situation?

422. How can you fix it?

423. Your best shot for providing estimations how complex/how much work does the activity require?

424. Schedule/cost recovery?

425. Are you working on the right risks?

426. Why do you need schedules?

2.20 Cost Management Plan: Holding Companies

427. Is there a set of procedures defining the scope, procedures, and deliverables defining quality control?

428. How does the proposed individual meet each requirement?

429. The definition of the Holding Companies project scope what needs to be accomplished?

430. Has the Holding Companies project scope been baselined?

431. Risk rating?

432. Has a capability assessment been conducted?

433. Are the quality tools and methods identified in the Quality Plan appropriate to the Holding Companies project?

434. Has a resource management plan been created?

435. Vac -variance at completion, how much over/ under budget do you expect to be?

436. Have all documents been archived in a Holding Companies project repository for each release?

437. Do Holding Companies project managers participating in the Holding Companies project know

the Holding Companies projects true status first hand?

438. Are schedule deliverables actually delivered?

439. What threats might prevent you from getting there?

440. Does all Holding Companies project documentation reside in a common repository for easy access?

441. Designated small business reserve?

442. Is the structure for tracking the Holding Companies project schedule well defined and assigned to a specific individual?

443. Has a provision been made to reassess Holding Companies project risks at various Holding Companies project stages?

444. Are updated Holding Companies project time & resource estimates reasonable based on the current Holding Companies project stage?

445. Is there general agreement & acceptance of the current status and progress of the Holding Companies project?

2.21 Activity Cost Estimates: Holding Companies

446. What makes a good expected result statement?

447. What is your organizations history in doing similar tasks?

448. What is Holding Companies project cost management?

449. What makes a good activity description?

450. Padding is bad and contingencies are good. what is the difference?

451. Were the tasks or work products prepared by the consultant useful?

452. Is costing method consistent with study goals?

453. How many activities should you have?

454. Can you change your activities?

455. What procedures are put in place regarding bidding and cost comparisons, if any?

456. Did the consultant work with local staff to develop local capacity?

457. Who & what determines the need for contracted services?

458. How do you allocate indirect costs to activities?

459. Were the costs or charges reasonable?

460. What is procurement?

461. If you are asked to lower your estimate because the price is too high, what are your options?

462. What communication items need improvement?

463. Did the Holding Companies project team have the right skills?

464. What is the activity inventory?

465. Measurable - are the targets measurable?

2.22 Cost Estimating Worksheet: Holding Companies

466. Will the Holding Companies project collaborate with the local community and leverage resources?

467. What is the purpose of estimating?

468. Value pocket identification & quantification what are value pockets?

469. What can be included?

470. Does the Holding Companies project provide innovative ways for stakeholders to overcome obstacles or deliver better outcomes?

471. Can a trend be established from historical performance data on the selected measure and are the criteria for using trend analysis or forecasting methods met?

472. Ask: are others positioned to know, are others credible, and will others cooperate?

473. How will the results be shared and to whom?

474. Who is best positioned to know and assist in identifying corresponding factors?

475. What is the estimated labor cost today based upon this information?

476. What will others want?

477. What happens to any remaining funds not used?

478. Is the Holding Companies project responsive to community need?

479. Is it feasible to establish a control group arrangement?

480. Identify the timeframe necessary to monitor progress and collect data to determine how the selected measure has changed?

481. What costs are to be estimated?

482. What info is needed?

483. What additional Holding Companies project(s) could be initiated as a result of this Holding Companies project?

2.23 Cost Baseline: Holding Companies

484. What is it ?

485. Has training and knowledge transfer of the operations organization been completed?

486. What weaknesses do you have?

487. Why do you manage cost?

488. Is request in line with priorities?

489. What is the consequence?

490. Have the actual milestone completion dates been compared to the approved schedule?

491. Have all the product or service deliverables been accepted by the customer?

492. Is the requested change request a result of changes in other Holding Companies project(s)?

493. Is the cr within Holding Companies project scope?

494. Should a more thorough impact analysis be conducted?

495. Have you identified skills that are missing from your team?

496. Has the actual cost of the Holding Companies project (or Holding Companies project phase) been tallied and compared to the approved budget?

497. Where do changes come from?

498. Will the Holding Companies project fail if the change request is not executed?

499. Does it impact schedule, cost, quality?

500. Holding Companies project goals -should others be reconsidered?

501. How will cost estimates be used?

502. Has the Holding Companies project documentation been archived or otherwise disposed as described in the Holding Companies project communication plan?

2.24 Quality Management Plan: Holding Companies

503. Would impacts defined serve as impediments?

504. How do you ensure that protocols are up to date?

505. Contradictory information between document sections?

506. How is staff trained in procedures?

507. What does it do for you (or to me)?

508. Methodology followed?

509. How do you decide what information needs to be recorded?

510. How are calibration records kept?

511. Checking the completeness and appropriateness of the sampling and testing. Were the right locations/samples tested for the right parameters?

512. Was trending evident between audits?

513. How do you field-modify testing procedures?

514. How do you manage quality?

515. How do you ensure that your sampling methods and procedures meet your data needs?

516. Are there procedures in place to effectively manage interdependencies with other Holding Companies projects / systems?

517. What is the Quality Management Plan?

518. No superfluous information or marketing narrative?

519. Are there nonconformance issues?

520. How does your organization use comparative data and information to improve organizational performance?

521. How do you document and correct nonconformances?

2.25 Quality Metrics: Holding Companies

522. Should a modifier be included?

523. Did evaluation start on time?

524. Are quality metrics defined?

525. Was material distributed on time?

526. Does risk analysis documentation meet standards?

527. Are there any open risk issues?

528. What do you measure?

529. What about still open problems?

530. What are you trying to accomplish?

531. There are many reasons to shore up quality-related metrics, and what metrics are important?

532. Have alternatives been defined in the event that failure occurs?

533. Were number of defects identified?

534. How does one achieve stability?

535. Is there alignment within your organization on

definitions?

536. What are your organizations next steps?

537. Is material complete (and does it meet the standards)?

538. How do you know if everyone is trying to improve the right things?

539. Filter visualizations of interest?

540. Has it met internal or external standards?

541. What is the benchmark?

2.26 Process Improvement Plan: Holding Companies

542. Does explicit definition of the measures exist?

543. What lessons have you learned so far?

544. Where do you focus?

545. Does your process ensure quality?

546. Are you meeting the quality standards?

547. Are you making progress on your improvement plan?

548. Have the frequency of collection and the points in the process where measurements will be made been determined?

549. Have the supporting tools been developed or acquired?

550. To elicit goal statements, do you ask a question such as, What do you want to achieve?

551. The motive is determined by asking, Why do you want to achieve this goal?

552. Have storage and access mechanisms and procedures been determined?

553. What personnel are the sponsors for that

initiative?

554. What personnel are the coaches for your initiative?

555. Where do you want to be?

556. How do you measure?

557. What makes people good SPI coaches?

558. Modeling current processes is great, and will you ever see a return on that investment?

2.27 Responsibility Assignment Matrix: Holding Companies

559. Changes in the current direct and Holding Companies projected base?

560. How many hours by each staff member/rate?

561. What can you do to improve productivity?

562. With too many people labeled as doing the work, are there too many hands involved?

563. Are material costs reported within the same period as that in which BCWP is earned for that material?

564. Is data disseminated to the contractors management timely, accurate, and usable?

565. Are people afraid to let you know when others are under allocated?

566. Do you know how your people are allocated?

567. Major functional areas of contract effort?

568. Are overhead costs budgets established on a basis consistent with anticipated direct business base?

569. Are the wbs and organizational levels for application of the Holding Companies projected

overhead costs identified?

570. What materials and procurements needed?

571. What expertise is available in your department?

572. Contract line items and end items?

573. Who is the Holding Companies project Manager?

574. When performing is split among two or more roles, is the work clearly defined so that the efforts are coordinated and the communication is clear?

575. Is every signing-off responsibility and every communicating responsibility critically necessary?

2.28 Roles and Responsibilities: Holding Companies

576. What should you do now to prepare for your career 5+ years from now?

577. Are governance roles and responsibilities documented?

578. Be specific; avoid generalities. Thank you and great work alone are insufficient. What exactly do you appreciate and why?

579. How is your work-life balance?

580. Are your policies supportive of a culture of quality data?

581. Authority: what areas/Holding Companies projects in your work do you have the authority to decide upon and act on the already stated decisions?

582. Was the expectation clearly communicated?

583. What is working well?

584. Is the data complete?

585. What should you do now to ensure that you are exceeding expectations and excelling in your current position?

586. Implementation of actions: Who are the

responsible units?

587. Does the team have access to and ability to use data analysis tools?

588. What should you do now to ensure that you are meeting all expectations of your current position?

589. Concern: where are you limited or have no authority, where you can not influence?

590. Who is responsible for each task?

591. How well did the Holding Companies project Team understand the expectations of specific roles and responsibilities?

592. What expectations were met?

593. Key conclusions and recommendations: Are conclusions and recommendations relevant and acceptable?

594. Once the responsibilities are defined for the Holding Companies project, have the deliverables, roles and responsibilities been clearly communicated to every participant?

2.29 Human Resource Management Plan: Holding Companies

595. Have reserves been created to address risks?

596. Were Holding Companies project team members involved in detailed estimating and scheduling?

597. Have lessons learned been conducted after each Holding Companies project release?

598. Is your organization primarily focused on a specific industry?

599. Is the Holding Companies project schedule available for all Holding Companies project team members to review?

600. How to convince employees that this is a necessary process?

601. Has a structured approach been used to break work effort into manageable components (WBS)?

602. Is there an approved case?

603. How will the Holding Companies project manage expectations & meet needs and requirements?

604. Is the manpower level sufficient to meet the future business requirements?

605. Has a Holding Companies project

Communications Plan been developed?

606. Are corrective actions and variances reported?

607. Has the schedule been baselined?

608. Are written status reports provided on a designated frequent basis?

609. Do you have the reasons why the changes to your organizational systems and capabilities are required?

610. Are Holding Companies project team members involved in detailed estimating and scheduling?

611. Were decisions made in a timely manner?

612. Have all documents been archived in a Holding Companies project repository for each release?

2.30 Communications Management Plan: Holding Companies

613. Can you think of other people who might have concerns or interests?

614. What does the stakeholder need from the team?

615. Where do team members get information?

616. Is the stakeholder role recognized by your organization?

617. Are others part of the communications management plan?

618. Who is responsible?

619. How much time does it take to do it?

620. What to know?

621. Is there an important stakeholder who is actively opposed and will not receive messages?

622. Who were proponents/opponents?

623. Do you feel a register helps?

624. Do you then often overlook a key stakeholder or stakeholder group?

625. Why is stakeholder engagement important?

626. Are you constantly rushing from meeting to meeting?

627. What approaches do you use?

628. Which stakeholders can influence others?

629. Are there common objectives between the team and the stakeholder?

630. In your work, how much time is spent on stakeholder identification?

631. Why manage stakeholders?

2.31 Risk Management Plan: Holding Companies

632. How is the audit profession changing?

633. Premium on reliability of product?

634. Are end-users enthusiastically committed to the Holding Companies project and the system/product to be built?

635. How will the Holding Companies project know if your organizations risk response actions were effective?

636. How much risk can you tolerate?

637. Financial risk -can your organization afford to undertake the Holding Companies project?

638. Are the best people available?

639. What is the likelihood that your organization would accept responsibility for the risk?

640. Is the customer willing to commit significant time to the requirements gathering process?

641. What are some questions that should be addressed in a risk management plan?

642. What is the probability the risk avoidance strategy will be successful?

643. Was an original risk assessment/risk management plan completed?

644. Is security a central objective?

645. Risk documentation: what reporting formats and processes will be used for risk management activities?

646. Do the people have the right combinations of skills?

647. Havent software Holding Companies projects been late before?

648. Where do risks appear in the business phases?

649. Does the Holding Companies project have the authority and ability to avoid the risk?

650. Do you manage the process through use of metrics?

651. Why do you need to manage Holding Companies project Risk?

2.32 Risk Register: Holding Companies

652. What evidence do you have to justify the likelihood score of the risk (audit, incident report, claim, complaints, inspection, internal review)?

653. What are you going to do to limit the Holding Companies projects risk exposure due to the identified risks?

654. What should the audit role be in establishing a risk management process?

655. How could corresponding Risk affect the Holding Companies project in terms of cost and schedule?

656. When will it happen?

657. What is the reason for current performance gaps and do the risks and opportunities identified previously account for this?

658. Are there other alternative controls that could be implemented?

659. Technology risk -is the Holding Companies project technically feasible?

660. What could prevent you delivering on the strategic program objectives and what is being done to mitigate corresponding issues?

661. When would you develop a risk register?

662. Cost/benefit – how much will the proposed mitigations cost and how does this cost compare with the potential cost of the risk event/situation should it occur?

663. Manageability – have mitigations to the risk been identified?

664. Contingency actions - planned actions to reduce the immediate seriousness of the risk when it does occur. What should you do when?

665. Budget and schedule: what are the estimated costs and schedules for performing risk-related activities?

666. What should you do when?

667. What are the main aims, objectives of the policy, strategy, or service and the intended outcomes?

668. What would the impact to the Holding Companies project objectives be should the risk arise?

669. Can the likelihood and impact of failing to achieve corresponding recommendations and action plans be assessed?

670. Are there any gaps in the evidence?

671. Does the evidence highlight any areas to advance opportunities or foster good relations. If yes what steps will be taken?

2.33 Probability and Impact Assessment: Holding Companies

672. Do you use diagramming techniques to show cause and effect?

673. Does the software interface with new or unproven hardware or unproven vendor products?

674. How is the risk management process used in practice?

675. What risks are necessary to achieve success?

676. Is the customer technically sophisticated in the product area?

677. Do requirements put excessive performance constraints on the product?

678. Monitoring of the overall Holding Companies project status – are there any changes in the Holding Companies project that can effect and cause new possible risks?

679. Are formal technical reviews part of this process?

680. Is a software Holding Companies project management tool available?

681. How are you working with risks?

682. Who should be notified of the occurrence of each

of the risk indicators?

683. What is the level of experience available with your organization?

684. How solid is the Holding Companies projection of competitive reaction?

685. Are enough people available?

686. What will be the likely political environment during the life of the Holding Companies project?

687. Does the software engineering team have the right mix of skills?

688. Who should be responsible for the monitoring and tracking of the indicators youhave identified?

689. How is the Holding Companies project going to be managed?

690. Are the risk data timely and relevant?

691. Can the Holding Companies project proceed without assuming the risk?

2.34 Probability and Impact Matrix: Holding Companies

692. Can you handle the investment risk?

693. How solid are the price-volume Holding Companies projections?

694. To what extent is the chosen technology maturing?

695. Who is going to be the consortium leader?

696. What will be the impact or consequence if the risk occurs?

697. Are testing tools available and suitable?

698. What are the risks involved in appointing external agencies to manage the Holding Companies project?

699. What lifestyle shifts might occur in society?

700. What would be the best solution?

701. Are the risk data complete?

702. What is the likelihood?

703. What are the likely future requirements?

704. Can you stabilize dynamic risk factors?

705. Costs associated with late delivery or a defective product?

706. Are Holding Companies project requirements stable?

707. Do you have specific methods that you use for each phase of the process?

708. Are some people working on multiple Holding Companies projects?

709. What should be done NEXT?

2.35 Risk Data Sheet: Holding Companies

710. What are the main opportunities available to you that you should grab while you can?

711. Potential for recurrence?

712. Whom do you serve (customers)?

713. What do you know?

714. How do you handle product safely?

715. Is the data sufficiently specified in terms of the type of failure being analyzed, and its frequency or probability?

716. How can hazards be reduced?

717. What can happen?

718. What will be the consequences if the risk happens?

719. What are you weak at and therefore need to do better?

720. What are you here for (Mission)?

721. What are you trying to achieve (Objectives)?

722. What can you do?

723. Has the most cost-effective solution been chosen?

724. What do people affected think about the need for, and practicality of preventive measures?

725. Do effective diagnostic tests exist?

726. What if client refuses?

727. What is the chance that it will happen?

2.36 Procurement Management Plan: Holding Companies

728. How will multiple providers be managed?

729. Are change requests logged and managed?

730. Have activity relationships and interdependencies within tasks been adequately identified?

731. Is the steering committee active in Holding Companies project oversight?

732. Are any non-compliance issues that exist communicated to your organization?

733. Similar Holding Companies projects?

734. Are parking lot items captured?

735. If standardized procurement documents are needed, where can others be found?

736. Public engagement – did you get it right?

737. Has your organization readiness assessment been conducted?

738. Does the detailed work plan match the complexity of tasks with the capabilities of personnel?

739. Does a documented Holding Companies project

organizational policy & plan (i.e. governance model) exist?

740. What is a Holding Companies project Management Plan?

2.37 Source Selection Criteria: Holding Companies

741. What are the most common types of rating systems?

742. How much weight should be placed on past performance information?

743. How is past performance evaluated?

744. What risks were identified in the proposals?

745. Are evaluators ready to begin this task?

746. What are the special considerations for preaward debriefings?

747. Team leads: what is your process for assigning ratings?

748. Who is entitled to a debriefing?

749. What will you use to capture evaluation and subsequent documentation?

750. How should oral presentations be evaluated?

751. Who must be notified?

752. Can you prevent comparison of proposals?

753. What should a DRFP include?

754. Does an evaluation need to include the identification of strengths and weaknesses?

755. When must you conduct a debriefing?

756. When is it appropriate to conduct a preproposal conference?

757. How will you evaluate offerors proposals?

758. Has all proposal data been loaded?

759. How do you ensure an integrated assessment of proposals?

760. What is the basis of an estimate and what assumptions were made?

2.38 Stakeholder Management Plan: Holding Companies

761. After observing execution of process, is it in compliance with the documented Plan?

762. Does the resource management plan include a personnel development plan?

763. What other teams / processes would be impacted by changes to the current process, and how?

764. How will you engage this stakeholder and gain commitment?

765. How are you doing/what can be done better?

766. Who is gathering information?

767. Has a quality assurance plan been developed for the Holding Companies project?

768. How much information should be collected?

769. Will the current technology alter during the life of the Holding Companies project?

770. Is an industry recognized mechanized support tool(s) being used for Holding Companies project scheduling & tracking?

771. What are the procedures and processes to be followed for purchases, including approval and

authorisation requirements?

772. What records are required (eg purchase orders, agreements)?

773. Are all key components of a Quality Assurance Plan present?

774. Is Holding Companies project status reviewed with the steering and executive teams at appropriate intervals?

775. Does the Holding Companies project have a Statement of Work?

776. Have all unresolved risks been documented?

777. Are milestone deliverables effectively tracked and compared to Holding Companies project plan?

2.39 Change Management Plan: Holding Companies

778. What is the negative impact of communicating too soon or too late?

779. What new behaviours are required?

780. What processes are in place to manage knowledge about the Holding Companies project?

781. Does this change represent a completely new process for your organization, or a different application of an existing process?

782. Why is the initiative is being undertaken - What are the business drivers?

783. Do there need to be new channels developed?

784. What communication network would you use – informal or formal?

785. What risks may occur upfront?

786. What policies and procedures need to be changed?

787. What type of materials/channels will be available to leverage?

788. Has the training co-ordinator been provided with the training details and put in place the necessary

arrangements?

789. What are the major changes to processes?

790. What does a resilient organization look like?

791. When does it make sense to customize?

792. Clearly articulate the overall business benefits of the Holding Companies project -why are you doing this now?

793. Impact of systems implementation on organization change?

794. What new competencies will be required for the roles?

795. What prerequisite knowledge do corresponding groups need?

796. Do you need a new organizational structure?

797. What work practices will be affected?

3.0 Executing Process Group: Holding Companies

798. Why is it important to determine activity sequencing on Holding Companies projects?

799. How will professionals learn what is expected from them what the deliverables are?

800. How is Holding Companies project performance information created and distributed?

801. How does Holding Companies project management relate to other disciplines?

802. What business situation is being addressed?

803. How can software assist in procuring goods and services?

804. Based on your Holding Companies project communication management plan, what worked well?

805. Are the necessary foundations in place to ensure the sustainability of the results of the programme?

806. How well did the chosen processes produce the expected results?

807. What good practices or successful experiences or transferable examples have been identified?

808. Are escalated issues resolved promptly?

809. Specific - is the objective clear in terms of what, how, when, and where the situation will be changed?

810. What are the main types of goods and services being outsourced?

811. It under budget or over budget?

812. Does software appear easy to learn?

813. What type of information goes in the quality assurance plan?

814. What are the challenges Holding Companies project teams face?

815. What are the typical Holding Companies project management skills?

3.1 Team Member Status Report: Holding Companies

816. What is to be done?

817. The problem with Reward & Recognition Programs is that the truly deserving people all too often get left out. How can you make it practical?

818. When a teams productivity and success depend on collaboration and the efficient flow of information, what generally fails them?

819. What specific interest groups do you have in place?

820. Does the product, good, or service already exist within your organization?

821. Do you have an Enterprise Holding Companies project Management Office (EPMO)?

822. Is there evidence that staff is taking a more professional approach toward management of your organizations Holding Companies projects?

823. How does this product, good, or service meet the needs of the Holding Companies project and your organization as a whole?

824. Does every department have to have a Holding Companies project Manager on staff?

825. Are the attitudes of staff regarding Holding Companies project work improving?

826. Why is it to be done?

827. Will the staff do training or is that done by a third party?

828. Does your organization have the means (staff, money, contract, etc.) to produce or to acquire the product, good, or service?

829. Are the products of your organizations Holding Companies projects meeting customers objectives?

830. How can you make it practical?

831. How will resource planning be done?

832. How much risk is involved?

833. How it is to be done?

834. Are your organizations Holding Companies projects more successful over time?

3.2 Change Request: Holding Companies

835. How are changes graded and who is responsible for the rating?

836. Has a formal technical review been conducted to assess technical correctness?

837. Who is responsible for the implementation and monitoring of all measures?

838. What is the change request log?

839. What type of changes does change control take into account?

840. How are the measures for carrying out the change established?

841. How fast will change requests be approved?

842. Will all change requests be unconditionally tracked through this process?

843. Are there requirements attributes that can discriminate between high and low reliability?

844. Are there requirements attributes that are strongly related to the complexity and size?

845. Does the schedule include Holding Companies project management time and change request

analysis time?

846. What should be regulated in a change control operating instruction?

847. What must be taken into consideration when introducing change control programs?

848. Who can suggest changes?

849. What is a Change Request Form?

850. Will this change conflict with other requirements changes (e.g., lead to conflicting operational scenarios)?

851. What kind of information about the change request needs to be captured?

852. Who is responsible to authorize changes?

853. What are the requirements for urgent changes?

3.3 Change Log: Holding Companies

854. When was the request submitted?

855. Will the Holding Companies project fail if the change request is not executed?

856. Is the submitted change a new change or a modification of a previously approved change?

857. Is this a mandatory replacement?

858. How does this change affect scope?

859. Is the requested change request a result of changes in other Holding Companies project(s)?

860. When was the request approved?

861. Does the suggested change request seem to represent a necessary enhancement to the product?

862. Is the change request open, closed or pending?

863. How does this relate to the standards developed for specific business processes?

864. How does this change affect the timeline of the schedule?

865. Who initiated the change request?

866. Is the change request within Holding Companies project scope?

867. Do the described changes impact on the integrity or security of the system?

868. Does the suggested change request represent a desired enhancement to the products functionality?

869. Is the change backward compatible without limitations?

3.4 Decision Log: Holding Companies

870. Adversarial environment. is your opponent open to a non-traditional workflow, or will it likely challenge anything you do?

871. What eDiscovery problem or issue did your organization set out to fix or make better?

872. What makes you different or better than others companies selling the same thing?

873. Who will be given a copy of this document and where will it be kept?

874. Do strategies and tactics aimed at less than full control reduce the costs of management or simply shift the cost burden?

875. Who is the decisionmaker?

876. Meeting purpose; why does this team meet?

877. Linked to original objective?

878. Which variables make a critical difference?

879. How effective is maintaining the log at facilitating organizational learning?

880. What was the rationale for the decision?

881. What are the cost implications?

882. With whom was the decision shared or considered?

883. What is your overall strategy for quality control / quality assurance procedures?

884. It becomes critical to track and periodically revisit both operational effectiveness; Are you noticing all that you need to, and are you interpreting what you see effectively?

885. How does the use a Decision Support System influence the strategies/tactics or costs?

886. Behaviors; what are guidelines that the team has identified that will assist them with getting the most out of team meetings?

887. What alternatives/risks were considered?

888. What is the average size of your matters in an applicable measurement?

889. How does an increasing emphasis on cost containment influence the strategies and tactics used?

3.5 Quality Audit: Holding Companies

890. Have the risks associated with the intentions been identified, analyzed and appropriate responses developed?

891. Health and safety arrangements; stress management workshops. How does your organization know that it provides a safe and healthy environment?

892. Is refuse and garbage adequately stored and disposed of with sufficient frequency to prevent contamination?

893. What is your organizations greatest strength?

894. How does your organization know that its promotions system is appropriately effective, constructive and fair?

895. Are storage areas and reconditioning operations designed to prevent mix-ups and assure orderly handling of both the distressed and reconditioned devices?

896. Are all employees made aware of device defects which may occur from the improper performance of specific jobs?

897. How does your organization know that its management system is appropriately effective and constructive?

898. How does your organization know that its

relationship with its (past) staff is appropriately effective and constructive?

899. What happens if your organization fails its Quality Audit?

900. Is there any content that may be legally actionable?

901. Statements of intent remain exactly that until they are put into effect. The next step is to deploy the already stated intentions. In other words, do the plans happen in reality?

902. How does your organization know that its general support services planning and management systems are appropriately effective and constructive?

903. How does your organization know that its system for governing staff behaviour is appropriately effective and constructive?

904. Are all employees including salespersons made aware that they must report all complaints received from any source for inclusion in the complaint handling system?

905. Are complaint files maintained?

906. What are your supplier audits?

907. Does your organization have set of goals, objectives, strategies and targets that are clearly understood by the Board and staff?

908. How does your organization know that its staff

financial services are appropriately effective and constructive?

909. What review processes are in place for your organizations major activities?

3.6 Team Directory: Holding Companies

910. What are you going to deliver or accomplish?

911. Process decisions: are there any statutory or regulatory issues relevant to the timely execution of work?

912. Why is the work necessary?

913. Process decisions: is work progressing on schedule and per contract requirements?

914. Process decisions: are contractors adequately prosecuting the work?

915. Where will the product be used and/or delivered or built when appropriate?

916. Decisions: is the most suitable form of contract being used?

917. When does information need to be distributed?

918. Timing: when do the effects of communication take place?

919. Who will be the stakeholders on your next Holding Companies project?

920. Contract requirements complied with?

921. Have you decided when to celebrate the Holding Companies projects completion date?

922. Process decisions: which organizational elements and which individuals will be assigned management functions?

923. Days from the time the issue is identified?

924. Decisions: what could be done better to improve the quality of the constructed product?

925. What needs to be communicated?

926. Does a Holding Companies project team directory list all resources assigned to the Holding Companies project?

927. How will the team handle changes?

3.7 Team Operating Agreement: Holding Companies

928. What resources can be provided for the team in terms of equipment, space, time for training, protected time and space for meetings, and travel allowances?

929. Do team members reside in more than two countries?

930. To whom do you deliver your services?

931. Are team roles clearly defined and accepted?

932. Have you established procedures that team members can follow to work effectively together, such as a team operating agreement?

933. Are there differences in access to communication and collaboration technology based on team member location?

934. How will your group handle planned absences?

935. Do you determine the meeting length and time of day?

936. What is a Virtual Team?

937. Are there influences outside the team that may affect performance, and if so, have you identified and addressed them?

938. Do you vary your voice pace, tone and pitch to engage participants and gain involvement?

939. Do you send out the agenda and meeting materials in advance?

940. What is culture?

941. What is the anticipated procedure (recruitment, solicitation of volunteers, or assignment) for selecting team members?

942. Confidentiality: how will confidential information be handled?

943. Must your members collaborate successfully to complete Holding Companies projects?

944. Methodologies: how will key team processes be implemented, such as training, research, work deliverable production, review and approval processes, knowledge management, and meeting procedures?

945. What is your unique contribution to your organization?

946. Do you post any action items, due dates, and responsibilities on the team website?

947. What are the current caseload numbers in the unit?

3.8 Team Performance Assessment: Holding Companies

948. Can team performance be reliably measured in simulator and live exercises using the same assessment tool?

949. Individual task proficiency and team process behavior: what is important for team functioning?

950. How much interpersonal friction is there in your team?

951. To what degree will the approach capitalize on and enhance the skills of all team members in a manner that takes into consideration other demands on members of the team?

952. Can familiarity breed backup?

953. Do friends perform better than acquaintances?

954. What structural changes have you made or are you preparing to make?

955. Does more radicalness mean more perceived benefits?

956. To what degree do the goals specify concrete team work products?

957. To what degree are the goals ambitious?

958. To what degree are the teams goals and objectives clear, simple, and measurable?

959. What are teams?

960. To what degree does the teams work approach provide opportunity for members to engage in results-based evaluation?

961. If you are worried about method variance before you collect data, what sort of design elements might you include to reduce or eliminate the threat of method variance?

962. To what degree does the teams work approach provide opportunity for members to engage in open interaction?

963. To what degree will the team adopt a concrete, clearly understood, and agreed-upon approach that will result in achievement of the teams goals?

964. How do you manage human resources?

965. To what degree can team members meet frequently enough to accomplish the teams ends?

966. To what degree are the goals realistic?

967. To what degree do team members understand one anothers roles and skills?

3.9 Team Member Performance Assessment: Holding Companies

968. What steps have you taken to improve performance?

969. How do you determine which data are the most important to use, analyze, or review?

970. What are acceptable governance changes?

971. How do you make use of research?

972. Why do performance reviews?

973. To what degree does the teams purpose contain themes that are particularly meaningful and memorable?

974. What is a general description of the processes under performance measurement and assessment?

975. To what degree can all members engage in open and interactive considerations?

976. What resources do you need?

977. How often are assessments to be conducted?

978. To what degree does the teams approach to its work allow for modification and improvement over time?

979. Should a ratee get a copy of all the raters documents about the employees performance?

980. How do you start collaborating?

981. How do you currently account for your results in the teams achievement?

982. Who they are?

983. Has the appropriate access to relevant data and analysis capability been granted?

984. What are the evaluation strategies (e.g., reaction, learning, behavior, results) used. What evaluation results did you have?

985. How will you identify your Team Leaders?

986. What are the standards or expectations for success?

987. Do the goals support your organizations goals?

3.10 Issue Log: Holding Companies

988. Why do you manage human resources?

989. How were past initiatives successful?

990. Who is the stakeholder?

991. What is the impact on the Business Case?

992. What effort will a change need?

993. Are they needed?

994. How do you manage communications?

995. What is the stakeholders political influence?

996. Do you have members of your team responsible for certain stakeholders?

997. Is the issue log kept in a safe place?

998. What is the status of the issue?

999. What is a Stakeholder?

1000. Who do you turn to if you have questions?

1001. Who reported the issue?

1002. What would have to change?

1003. Which team member will work with each

stakeholder?

1004. What date was the issue resolved?

4.0 Monitoring and Controlling Process Group: Holding Companies

1005. Is there sufficient time allotted between the general system design and the detailed system design phases?

1006. What is the timeline?

1007. Propriety: who needs to be involved in the evaluation to be ethical?

1008. Key stakeholders to work with. How many potential communications channels exist on the Holding Companies project?

1009. Who needs to be involved in the planning?

1010. Does the solution fit in with organizations technical architectural requirements?

1011. How do you monitor progress?

1012. How is agile program management done?

1013. What are the goals of the program?

1014. Is there undesirable impact on staff or resources?

1015. Is the program in place as intended?

1016. What departments are involved in its daily

operation?

1017. What do they need to know about the Holding Companies project?

1018. How many more potential communications channels were introduced by the discovery of the new stakeholders?

1019. How to ensure validity, quality and consistency?

1020. What were things that you need to improve?

1021. User: who wants the information and what are they interested in?

1022. Feasibility: how much money, time, and effort can you put into this?

4.1 Project Performance Report: Holding Companies

1023. To what degree do the structures of the formal organization motivate taskrelevant behavior and facilitate task completion?

1024. To what degree does the teams work approach provide opportunity for members to engage in fact-based problem solving?

1025. To what degree is the information network consistent with the structure of the formal organization?

1026. To what degree does the information network communicate information relevant to the task?

1027. What is the PRS?

1028. To what degree can the team measure progress against specific goals?

1029. To what degree does the funding match the requirement?

1030. To what degree is the team cognizant of small wins to be celebrated along the way?

1031. To what degree do all members feel responsible for all agreed-upon measures?

1032. To what degree does the task meet individual

needs?

1033. To what degree will new and supplemental skills be introduced as the need is recognized?

1034. To what degree are the demands of the task compatible with and converge with the mission and functions of the formal organization?

1035. To what degree does the team possess adequate membership to achieve its ends?

1036. To what degree are the members clear on what they are individually responsible for and what they are jointly responsible for?

1037. Next Steps?

4.2 Variance Analysis: Holding Companies

1038. Are overhead cost budgets established for each department which has authority to incur overhead costs?

1039. What costs are avoidable if one or more customers are dropped?

1040. What is the budgeted cost for work scheduled?

1041. Is the market likely to continue to grow at this rate next year?

1042. Did an existing competitor change strategy?

1043. Are there externalities from having some customers, even if they are unprofitable in the short run?

1044. What was the cause of the increase in costs?

1045. Can the contractor substantiate work package and planning package budgets?

1046. Are procedures for variance analysis documented and consistently applied at the control account level and selected WBS and organizational levels at least monthly as a routine task?

1047. What are the actual costs to date?

1048. What does a favorable labor efficiency variance mean?

1049. Are records maintained to show how management reserves are used?

1050. Is the entire contract planned in time-phased control accounts to the extent practicable?

1051. What types of services and expense are shared between business segments?

1052. Other relevant issues of Variance Analysis -selling price or gross margin?

1053. What causes selling price variance?

1054. At what point should variances be isolated and brought to the attention of the management?

4.3 Earned Value Status: Holding Companies

1055. If earned value management (EVM) is so good in determining the true status of a Holding Companies project and Holding Companies project its completion, why is it that hardly any one uses it in information systems related Holding Companies projects?

1056. How much is it going to cost by the finish?

1057. Are you hitting your Holding Companies projects targets?

1058. Verification is a process of ensuring that the developed system satisfies the stakeholders agreements and specifications; Are you building the product right? What do you verify?

1059. Validation is a process of ensuring that the developed system will actually achieve the stakeholders desired outcomes; Are you building the right product? What do you validate?

1060. How does this compare with other Holding Companies projects?

1061. Where is evidence-based earned value in your organization reported?

1062. When is it going to finish?

1063. What is the unit of forecast value?

1064. Earned value can be used in almost any Holding Companies project situation and in almost any Holding Companies project environment. it may be used on large Holding Companies projects, medium sized Holding Companies projects, tiny Holding Companies projects (in cut-down form), complex and simple Holding Companies projects and in any market sector. some people, of course, know all about earned value, they have used it for years - but perhaps not as effectively as they could have?

1065. Where are your problem areas?

4.4 Risk Audit: Holding Companies

1066. Do you have proper induction processes for all new paid staff and volunteers who have a specific role and responsibility?

1067. Does your auditor understand your business?

1068. To what extent should analytical procedures be utilized in the risk-assessment process?

1069. Do you meet the legislative requirements (for example PAYG, super contributions) for paid employees?

1070. What events or circumstances could affect the achievement of your objectives?

1071. Will an appropriate standard of care be applied to all involved?

1072. Do you promote education and training opportunities?

1073. Does the customer have a solid idea of what is required?

1074. Are staff committed for the duration of the product?

1075. Does your organization have an up-to-date constitution?

1076. Have you reviewed your constitution within the

last twelve months?

1077. Have all involved been advised of any obligations they have to sponsors?

1078. What are risks and how do you manage them?

1079. Do you have an understanding of insurance claims processes?

1080. Are Holding Companies project requirements stable?

1081. What effect would a better risk management program have had?

1082. Are you aware of the industry standards that apply to your operations?

1083. Do you have an emergency plan?

1084. How can the strategy fail/achieved?

1085. What programmatic and Fiscal information is being collected and analyzed?

4.5 Contractor Status Report: Holding Companies

1086. What process manages the contracts?

1087. What was the final actual cost?

1088. What was the budget or estimated cost for your organizations services?

1089. What was the overall budget or estimated cost?

1090. Describe how often regular updates are made to the proposed solution. Are corresponding regular updates included in the standard maintenance plan?

1091. Who can list a Holding Companies project as organization experience, your organization or a previous employee of your organization?

1092. How is risk transferred?

1093. What is the average response time for answering a support call?

1094. What are the minimum and optimal bandwidth requirements for the proposed solution?

1095. What was the actual budget or estimated cost for your organizations services?

1096. If applicable; describe your standard schedule for new software version releases. Are new software version releases included in the standard maintenance plan?

1097. Are there contractual transfer concerns?

1098. How long have you been using the services?

4.6 Formal Acceptance: Holding Companies

1099. General estimate of the costs and times to complete the Holding Companies project?

1100. Who would use it?

1101. Was the client satisfied with the Holding Companies project results?

1102. Who supplies data?

1103. Does it do what client said it would?

1104. How well did the team follow the methodology?

1105. Was the Holding Companies project work done on time, within budget, and according to specification?

1106. What function(s) does it fill or meet?

1107. What is the Acceptance Management Process?

1108. Did the Holding Companies project manager and team act in a professional and ethical manner?

1109. Was the Holding Companies project goal achieved?

1110. Do you perform formal acceptance or burn-in tests?

1111. What can you do better next time?

1112. What lessons were learned about your Holding Companies project management methodology?

1113. Do you buy pre-configured systems or build your own configuration?

1114. Did the Holding Companies project achieve its MOV?

1115. What features, practices, and processes proved to be strengths or weaknesses?

1116. What are the requirements against which to test, Who will execute?

1117. Was business value realized?

1118. Do you buy-in installation services?

5.0 Closing Process Group: Holding Companies

1119. Is this a follow-on to a previous Holding Companies project?

1120. Were the outcomes different from the already stated planned?

1121. Was the schedule met?

1122. What do you need to do?

1123. Just how important is your work to the overall success of the Holding Companies project?

1124. How will staff learn how to use the deliverables?

1125. What were things that you did well, and could improve, and how?

1126. Does the close educate others to improve performance?

1127. Did you do things well?

1128. What is the Holding Companies project name and date of completion?

1129. What areas were overlooked on this Holding Companies project?

1130. What were the desired outcomes?

1131. Is the Holding Companies project funded?

1132. Mitigate. what will you do to minimize the impact should a risk event occur?

1133. What areas were overlooked on this Holding Companies project?

1134. What can you do better next time, and what specific actions can you take to improve?

1135. Are there funding or time constraints?

5.1 Procurement Audit: Holding Companies

1136. Does the procurement function/unit have the ability to negotiate with customers and suppliers?

1137. Are travel expenditures monitored to determine that they are in line with other employees and reasonable for the area of travel?

1138. Have guidelines incorporating the principles and objectives of a robust procurement practice been established?

1139. Are the journals and ledgers kept current for all funds?

1140. Does the procurement Holding Companies project have a clear goal and does the goal meet the specified needs of the users?

1141. Does procurement staff have recognized professional procurement qualifications or sufficient training?

1142. Are procurement processes well organized and documented?

1143. Is there no evidence of collusion between bidders?

1144. Does the procurement function/unit have the ability to secure best performance from contractors?

1145. Does procurement staff have skills to procure complex or special items (i.e. IT)?

1146. Are all purchase orders accounted for?

1147. Are the pages of the minutes book press pre-numbered?

1148. Months to reflect any changes in policy?

1149. Is trend analysis performed on expenditures made by key employees and by vendor?

1150. Were products/services not received within the prescribed time limit?

1151. Are all pre-numbered checks accounted for on a regular basis?

1152. Are advantages and disadvantages of in-house production, outsourcing and Public Private Partnerships considered?

1153. Was the award decision based on the result of the evaluation of tenders?

1154. Is there no evidence of favouritism towards a particular contractor during the evaluation and negotiation processes?

1155. Does the individual having check-signing responsibility review the use of the signature plates?

5.2 Contract Close-Out: Holding Companies

1156. Have all acceptance criteria been met prior to final payment to contractors?

1157. Change in knowledge?

1158. Change in circumstances?

1159. Have all contract records been included in the Holding Companies project archives?

1160. How does it work?

1161. Was the contract sufficiently clear so as not to result in numerous disputes and misunderstandings?

1162. Parties: Authorized?

1163. How is the contracting office notified of the automatic contract close-out?

1164. Has each contract been audited to verify acceptance and delivery?

1165. Change in attitude or behavior?

1166. Are the signers the authorized officials?

1167. What happens to the recipient of services?

1168. Was the contract type appropriate?

1169. What is capture management?

1170. How/when used ?

1171. Have all contracts been closed?

1172. Parties: who is involved?

1173. Was the contract complete without requiring numerous changes and revisions?

1174. Have all contracts been completed?

5.3 Project or Phase Close-Out: Holding Companies

1175. What is this stakeholder expecting?

1176. Is the lesson based on actual Holding Companies project experience rather than on independent research?

1177. In preparing the Lessons Learned report, should it reflect a consensus viewpoint, or should the report reflect the different individual viewpoints?

1178. What information did each stakeholder need to contribute to the Holding Companies projects success?

1179. Does the lesson educate others to improve performance?

1180. What was expected from each stakeholder?

1181. What are the marketing communication needs for each stakeholder?

1182. What information is each stakeholder group interested in?

1183. Who controlled key decisions that were made?

1184. Have business partners been involved extensively, and what data was required for them?

1185. What are they?

1186. If you were the Holding Companies project sponsor, how would you determine which Holding Companies project team(s) and/or individuals deserve recognition?

1187. Were messages directly related to the release strategy or phases of the Holding Companies project?

1188. When and how were information needs best met?

1189. Planned completion date?

1190. What hierarchical authority does the stakeholder have in your organization?

1191. Were risks identified and mitigated?

1192. Who controlled the resources for the Holding Companies project?

1193. Who exerted influence that has positively affected or negatively impacted the Holding Companies project?

1194. What could be done to improve the process?

5.4 Lessons Learned: Holding Companies

1195. Was sufficient advance training conducted and/or information provided to enable the already stated affected by the changes to adjust to and accommodate them?

1196. How effectively and timely was your organizational change impact identified and planned for?

1197. What is the fiscal dependency?

1198. Were quality procedures built into the Holding Companies project?

1199. Were the aims and objectives achieved?

1200. How much time is required for the task?

1201. Are lessons learned documented?

1202. What is the economic growth rate?

1203. Why do you need to measure?

1204. How effective was the support you received during implementation of the product/service?

1205. What needs to be done over or differently?

1206. Was the change control process properly

implemented to manage changes to cost, scope, schedule, or quality?

1207. Does the lesson describe a function that would be done differently the next time?

1208. What were the success factors?

1209. What is the value of the deliverable?

1210. What is the growth stage of your organization?

1211. What did you do right?

1212. What is the growth stage of the organization?

1213. What were the major enablers to a quick response?

Index

estimates   3-4, 32, 46, 58, 136-137, 151, 167, 171, 174-175, 180
estimating   4, 154-155, 169, 177, 191-192
estimation   75, 133
etcetera   43, 112
ethical 17, 118, 236, 248
ethnic 115
evaluate   73, 78, 82, 145, 208
evaluated   207
evaluating   74
evaluation   58, 82, 84, 88, 183, 207-208, 231, 233, 236, 253
evaluators   207
events 19, 73, 79-80, 128, 244
everyday   64
everyone   27, 30, 184
everything   47
evidence   10, 50, 197-198, 215, 252-253
evident   181
evolution   42
evolve 92
exactly 189, 224
examined   35
example   2, 8, 12, 15, 61, 93, 244
examples   7-8, 213
exceed   149, 162
exceeding   54, 189
excellence   7, 33
excellent   51
excelling   189
excessive   154, 199
execute   249
executed   180, 219
Executing   5, 213
execution   95, 209, 226
executive   7, 102, 128, 210
executives   117
Exercise   22, 162
exercises   230
exerted   257
existing 9, 93, 122, 136, 139, 146, 211, 240
expect 118, 170, 173
expected   24, 28, 82, 104, 119, 167, 175, 213, 256
expecting   256

inclusion   224
increase   74, 118, 167, 240
increased   113
increasing   106, 222
incurred   44
incurring   152
in-depth   8, 10
indicate   64, 91, 121
indicated   90
indicators   52, 57, 61, 63, 70, 77, 134, 200
indirect   52, 151-152, 176
indirectly   1
individual   1, 49, 170, 173-174, 230, 238, 253, 256
induction   244
industry   92, 108, 191, 209, 245
infinite 119
influence   111, 126, 130, 132, 190, 194, 222, 234, 257
influences   160, 228
informal   211
ingrained   93
in-house   128, 253
initial   35, 121
initially 38
initiated   178, 219
initiating   2, 109, 126, 148
initiative   10, 186, 211
Innovate   72
innovation   49, 68, 73, 88, 101, 111, 160
innovative   112, 177
in-process   70
inputs   32, 37, 47, 60, 94, 126
inside   24
insight 59, 71
insights 8
inspection   197
inspired   109
Instead110
insurance   245
insure   105
integrate   76, 95, 123
integrated   208
integrity   22, 120, 220
intended   1, 80, 198, 236

INTENT 15, 26, 42, 56, 72, 87, 100, 224
intention   1
intentions   223-224
interact   120
interest 101, 184, 215
interested   132, 237, 256
interests   23, 193
interface   199
interim 112
internal   1, 37, 57, 121, 127, 131, 153, 184, 197
interpret   10
intervals   210
interview   101
introduced   237, 239
invalid 154
inventory   176
invest 68
investment   49, 62, 186, 201
investor   53
involve 106
involved   18, 20, 34, 47, 59, 122, 167, 187, 191-192, 201,
216, 236, 244-245, 255-256
involves   91
isolated   241
issues   17, 19-20, 23-24, 128, 137-138, 142, 146, 162, 164, 182-
183, 197, 205, 214, 226, 241
itself   1, 23
jointly   239
journals   252
judgment   1
justified96, 127, 147
justify   197
killer   112
knowledge   9, 27, 37, 77, 82, 88-89, 94, 97-98, 104, 108, 114,
131, 179, 211-212, 229, 254
labeled   187
lacked 92
largely 63
latest   8
leader 19, 60, 67, 77, 201
leaders30, 65, 68, 92, 103, 111, 233
leadership   22, 34-35, 73, 103, 110
learned   6, 98, 116, 185, 191, 249, 256, 258

mechanical   1
mechanisms   134, 185
mechanized   209
medium   243
meeting   32-33, 91, 138, 146, 185, 190, 194, 216, 221, 228-229
meetings   32-33, 39, 140, 222, 228
megatrends   106
member   5, 35, 110, 187, 215, 228, 232, 234
members   27-28, 69, 94, 139, 191-193, 228-232, 234, 238-239
membership   239
memorable   232
message   91
messages   193, 257
method   42, 133, 135, 145, 159, 168, 175, 231
methods   31-32, 49, 60, 135, 173, 177, 181, 202
metrics 4, 28, 62, 97, 128, 137, 140, 183, 196
milestone   3, 128, 137, 160, 179, 210
milestones   31, 130, 158
minimize   133, 171, 251
minimizing   59, 103
minimum   246
minority   23
minutes   32, 75, 253
missed 44, 115
missing 61, 104, 159, 179
mission 61, 70, 112, 119, 203, 239
mitigate   85, 197, 251
mitigated   257
mitigation   135
mix-ups   223
Modeling   63, 186
models 22, 47, 59, 118
modified   94
modifier   183
module   171
moment   120
moments   69
momentum   106, 115
monetary   20
monitor   88, 90, 92, 98, 178, 236
monitored   93, 95-96, 156, 169, 252
monitoring   5, 88, 94-97, 155, 164, 199-200, 217, 236

presented   23
preserve   33
preserved   66
pressures   160
prevent   53, 155, 174, 197, 207, 223
preventive   204
prevents   19
previous   37, 246, 250
previously   197, 219
primarily   191
primary   165
principles   134, 252
priorities   42, 47-48, 50, 179
priority 46, 54, 158
privacy   30, 135
Private 253
probably   165
problem   15, 17, 20-27, 31, 37, 45, 53, 61, 140, 142, 215, 221, 238, 243
problems   16, 18, 20-21, 25, 75, 82, 84, 90, 113, 142, 183
procedure   229
procedures   9, 82, 89, 93, 95-96, 138, 152, 164, 173, 175, 181-182, 185, 209, 211, 222, 228-229, 240, 244, 258
proceed   200
proceeding   169
process   1-7, 9, 27, 29, 32-34, 37, 43, 56-63, 65-70, 89-91, 93-95, 98, 126-128, 133, 139, 142-143, 145-148, 164, 167, 185, 191, 195-197, 199, 202, 207, 209, 211, 213, 217, 226-227, 230, 236, 242, 244, 246, 248, 250, 257-258
processes   44, 49, 57, 59-60, 64-68, 70, 88, 93, 97, 133, 137, 145, 153-154, 186, 196, 209, 211-213, 219, 225, 229, 232, 244-245, 249, 252-253
procure   253
procuring   213
produce   57, 126, 129, 164, 213, 216
produced   64, 75
produces   159
producing   143, 145
product   1, 49, 61, 63, 112, 119, 140, 146, 160-161, 179, 195, 199, 202-203, 215-216, 219, 226-227, 242, 244, 258
production   35, 86, 113, 229, 253
products   1, 15, 19, 51, 118, 134, 143, 175, 199, 216, 220, 230, 253

rephrased   9
replace   45
replacing   139
Report 5-6, 85, 88, 197, 215, 224, 238, 246, 256
reported   151, 187, 192, 234, 242
reporting   60, 93, 110, 196
reports 55, 94, 130, 153, 192
repository   173-174, 192
represent   79, 211, 219-220
reproduced   1
reputation   103
request   5, 61, 139, 179-180, 217-220
requested   1, 126, 179, 219
requests   205, 217
require 32, 45, 57, 60, 93-94, 129, 164, 172
required   15, 27-28, 35, 37, 39, 61, 67, 74, 81, 92, 126-127,
134, 141, 151, 156, 158, 168-169, 192, 210-212, 244, 256, 258
requiring   130, 255
research   22, 108, 112, 132, 229, 232, 256
reserve 174
reserved   1
reserves   191, 241
reside 79, 174, 228
resilient212
resolution   59, 73
resolve 20, 24
resolved   137, 214, 235
resource   3-4, 100, 154, 158, 164-166, 168, 173-174, 191,
209, 216
resources   2, 7, 15-16, 23, 25, 27, 39, 50, 69, 81, 88, 92, 97,
100, 108, 112, 119, 126-127, 131, 140, 151, 156, 158, 163, 166,
168, 177, 227-228, 231-232, 234, 236, 257
respect   1
respond   133
responded   11
response   18-19, 22, 90-91, 95, 98, 195, 246, 259
responses   80, 108, 223
responsive   178
result   75, 79, 146, 175, 178-179, 219, 231, 253-254
resulted   90
resulting   57
results 8, 28-29, 63, 72-74, 77, 80-82, 85, 90, 126, 134, 137, 151,
167, 177, 213, 233, 248

standards   1, 9-10, 88, 90, 93, 96, 138, 147, 183-185, 219, 233, 245
started 8, 160, 163
starting9
stated 111-112, 151-152, 167, 189, 224, 250, 258
statement   3, 10, 75, 84, 145, 175, 210
statements   11, 25, 31, 37, 41, 55, 71, 86, 99, 124, 139, 167, 185, 224
status 5-6, 63, 126, 152, 154, 174, 192, 199, 210, 215, 234, 242, 246
statutory   226
steady 43
steering   148, 205, 210
stopper   141
storage   185, 223
stored 223
stories 31
strategic   42, 78, 95, 112, 197
strategies   77, 106, 111, 133, 221-222, 224, 233
strategy   25, 41, 47, 73, 76, 79, 100, 112, 114, 123, 133, 147, 154, 195, 198, 222, 240, 245, 257
Stream 58, 64
strength   223
strengths   131, 147, 208, 249
stress   223
stretch 114
strict   58
strive   114
Strongly   10, 15, 26, 42, 56, 72, 87, 100, 217
structural   230
structure   3, 78, 104, 122, 145, 149, 165, 174, 212, 238
structured   113, 191
structures   238
stubborn   106
stupid 120
subject8-9, 35
subjective   139
subjects   66
submitted   219
subsequent   207
subset 21
succeed   49, 117

Made in the USA
Monee, IL
24 May 2023

34501258R00176